MONEY
Athletics

MONEYLETICS
MAP
SERIES

MONEY
Athletics

YOUR GAME PLAN TO A
FINANCIALLY FIT TWEEN

CRAIG KALEY

Money Athletics: Your Game Plan to a Financially Fit Tween
Published by Left Lane Publishing
Parker, CO

Library of Congress Control Number: 2017940018

ISBN: 978-0-9989211-0-5

FAMILY & RELATIONSHIPS / Parenting
BUSINESS & ECONOMICS / Personal Finance / Money Management
EDUCATION / Finance

QUANTITY PURCHASES: Schools, companies, professional groups, clubs, and other organizations may qualify for special terms when ordering quantities of this title. For information, email info@LeftLanePublishing.com.

This book is dedicated to my wife, Karen,
and our kids, Scott, Nicole, and Tyler.
God has blessed me with all of you
and the inspiration to embark on this project
to help other families.

MONEYLETICS MAP SERIES

The Moneyletics MAP Series has been developed as a progression of books and corresponding programs to teach children about money as they grow through the stages of childhood into adulthood. The Moneyletics MAP Series includes the following:

- Money Amateurs Program
  (for young children to age ten)
- Money Athletics Program
  (for tweens from ages eleven to fourteen)
- Money All-Stars Program
  (for teenagers from ages fifteen to eighteen)
- Money All-Stars Plus
  (for young adults from age eighteen forward)

Contents

THE WORLD IS OUT TO GET US FINANCIALLY

During the summer of 2007, just before the great recession kicked off, I was about to return home from a business trip in San Francisco. Unfortunately, my return flight was canceled at the last minute due to mechanical issues. The next flight left me waiting seven hours in the airport. I remembered walking past a barber in the airport earlier, so I decided to make the best of the situation and return to get a haircut.

Although I did not have an appointment, Stephanie was available to cut my hair. I learned through our conversation that Stephanie was a twenty-six-year-old woman who had a young son. In addition to cutting hair, she also worked as a server at a popular restaurant in the city. The reason I remember this conversation so well is that on the counter next to her station, Stephanie had a pile of house listings that she had printed off and was reviewing during her breaks between customers.

We talked about the houses she was considering. All of them had price tags greater than $500,000 and as high as $800,000. I remember thinking to myself, *How can a young woman who works as a server and hair stylist afford to buy such an expensive home? Did she come from money?* Stephanie told me that Keith, her real estate broker, had said that buying real estate was not only easy, but the sooner she jumped into the market, the sooner she could provide for herself and her son. To calm her fears about buying an expensive home, Keith had explained, "Stephanie, real estate never goes down in value. It always appreciates." She would not even need to prove that her income could support the payments. This was during a period when lenders offered what were called "no documentation loans." The issue was that these loans not only put the borrower in jeopardy, but they also provided great commissions to the people who sold them. As a result, Keith was motivated to have Stephanie take on such a loan since he would receive a good payday regardless of her capacity to manage such a large mortgage.

It turned out that Stephanie did not come from money. Nor was she knowledgeable about some of the basics of finance, much less the complexities of mortgages. She was not yet a financially fit young adult, yet she was contemplating a significant life-changing financial decision. I can only hope that things turned out OK for Stephanie, but the odds were against her.

This book, intended for youth between the ages of eleven and fourteen, which I define as "tweens," is not specifically about teaching our children how to recognize the Keiths of the world. It is about how to strengthen their knowledge and confidence so that when they become young adults they will be financially self-assured in that they will know how to own their money situation, steer away from trouble, and remain on solid financial footing.

WHY THIS BOOK IS DIFFERENT FROM THE REST

Many of us have heard the definition of insanity attributed to Albert Einstein:

"Insanity—Doing the same thing over and over again and expecting different results."

Have you noticed that many of our approaches to raising financially fit youth and young adults feel like they fit this definition? For example, whether it is a book, seminar, or class at school, they all seem to have one thing in common. They are missing a key ingredient with regard to teaching personal finance.

Whatever the program or system, they all seem to explain the concepts of earning money, saving money, budgeting, debt, interest rates, and so on. Many of these sources have great approaches to explain those concepts and even offer examples and exercises to help learners deepen their understanding. Those elements are important in an overall program; however, I do not think that they alone will provide a solid financial base of knowledge and skills for your children and their future.

In my opinion, the missing ingredient in these programs is a feedback mechanism to solidify that content. What is needed is an ongoing feedback loop to create an environment where your children can practice those skills every single day in the real world, not just for the time it takes them to complete the book, seminar, or class. The skills learned must be relevant and applicable for the rest of their lives.

GROWING FINANCIALLY FIT TWEENS

Would you embark on a new fitness program without a plan? Would you take up a new sport without some guidance and practice? Most likely not.

Growing your tweens into financially fit young adults is more achievable if you approach their growth in managing money much like you would approach their growth as an athlete. Let's say your tweens want to run a marathon, excel on the swim team, or elevate their game on the soccer or baseball field. Depending upon their desires, you would help them achieve their goal by providing them with coaching—either from you or from an expert in the sport—to introduce new skills and help them hone those skills into habits. In order to achieve mastery, a lot of practice is necessary. The same is true for your tweens if they are going to develop as money athletes. They need to be coached in money skills and provided an environment in which to practice those skills so that the behaviors become habits.

In the past, teaching kids about money was done using

cash. That is still probably true for kids ten years old and younger. However, for preteens and teenagers, a cash-only operating environment is "old school" and may put them at a disadvantage when they reach adulthood. Today's youth purchase their music via services such as iTunes. They shop on Amazon or an endless number of other websites. None of these sites or services accept cash. They rely on credit cards, debit cards, and services such as PayPal. Many stores even allow payments through smartphones. Interestingly, articles have begun to surface on the topic of "the end of cash." I don't believe a cash-free society will be upon us in the near future, but cash may become a rarity within the next twenty to thirty years.

The Aha Moment!

I would like to say that I woke up one day with an epiphany of a better way to instruct my children about money. In actuality, it did not happen like that. Rather, it's been a journey that has encompassed more than ten years so far—one that has inspired me both as a parent and as a believer in our younger generations.

The spark of this program started ten years ago when my son Scott, who was twelve at the time, came up to me while I was entering information from my paycheck stub into Quicken, the personal finance program I used at the time to track our family finances. Here's how the conversation went:

"Dad, what are you doing?"

"I am entering information from my paycheck into Quicken," I replied.

Scott was very inquisitive for his young age, and we proceeded to discuss at a high level the concepts of salary, insurance deductions, a 401(k) retirement plan, charitable contributions, and yes, even taxes. You can probably imagine how this conversation went.

"What is salary?"

"Salary is what I receive for the work I do."

"What is insurance?"

The question-and-answer sequence went on for about fifteen minutes. I have to say that the conversation was a fun opportunity for exploration between my son and me. And the statement he made at the end of our discussion is what sparked a thought in me.

"Dad, I can't wait until I can get a paycheck!"

I wanted to capitalize on my son's excitement and wondered how I could do that. After this conversation, I started to ponder whether there was a way to set up a program that would allow my kids to experience the personal finance foundations they would need as adults, including "getting a paycheck." I didn't want it to be a make-believe game, but one that practiced real-world concepts. I wanted them to feel confident and empowered so that when they found themselves in a situation like Stephanie experienced, they would be able to make the right decisions.

At the time, I coached my kids in multiple sports, including soccer and baseball. Additionally, I had taught them to ski and snowboard. Common to all of this coaching were the teaching part, the coaching and guiding part, and finally, the practice, practice, and practice part. It seemed that if I could apply the elements of athletic coaching to the development of money skills, I would be able to ignite a better way for them to understand and manage their money in the future.

THE BIRTH OF THE MONEY ATHLETICS PROGRAM

That pondering blossomed into our ten-year journey and the development of the Money Athletics Program and this book. The following chapters will lead you through what I used with our kids and will show you how to develop your own Money Athletics Program for your tween. Your son or daughter will experience what it is like to receive a paycheck and learn the responsibility of making purchase decisions. He or she will learn the importance of saving and investing and how those decisions made today will affect their tomorrow. I will also share with you the benefits of including a charitable facet to your program. And I will not be shy about telling you where I made some mistakes in the program I set up with my children, as well as where we laughed and even enjoyed some inspirational moments.

Like me, you will find your own unique ways to teach financial concepts to your tweens, and you will learn new things along the way. This book will certainly guide you through the program, but like riding a bike, at some point you will not have someone holding your bicycle and running beside you. By the end of *Money Athletics,* you will be off and riding on your own.

CONFIRMATION OF THE RIGHT PATH!

We happened to roll out this program to our children Scott and Nicole in the month of December. Earlier in the month, our kids had brought home from school the hot lunch menu for January. We always had to select not only the number of hot lunches they wanted each week, but also the specific days of the week they wanted to have a hot lunch during the next month. Our rule at the time was that they could have two hot lunches a week. On the other three days, they had to bring their own lunch in a lunch box or lunch bag.

This ratio seemed to work well since our kids did not like all of the food provided by the school. For example, I seem to remember that the school's macaroni with cheese was not to their liking, so they never chose that lunch. Although we didn't have to turn in the forms until the third week of December for January's lunch order, Scott and Nicole went ahead and made their selections early in the month, leaving us the final task of handing in the forms a couple of weeks later. As part of the financial plan we intended to roll out to our children that December, when it came time to pay for the hot lunches, each of our kids would be able to write a check for the hot lunches. Seemed straightforward to us!

We rolled out the program with a lot of excitement around it. To be honest, at the time I was not sure what would really happen, so I was a bit nervous not knowing how our kids would react. Imagine the look on the faces of a twelve- and eleven-year-old when they were told they would be managing their own money. Yes, they had big eyes and huge smiles! Because it was close to Christmas, we knew that toys were on their minds and considered that they might want to spend all of their money on playthings. *Was I going to regret this?* Just a day after we rolled out the program, we asked both Scott and Nicole if they were still on board with the hot lunches they'd selected for January. We reminded them that they would be required to write a check each month to cover the cost of their lunches as part of the money they would be managing for themselves. That is when the questions started.

"You mean I have to write a check each month for hot lunches?" one of them asked.

"Yes," I replied. "It is what we agreed to. You are responsible for covering various expenses, including your hot lunches."

"We are not sure we want to have hot lunches then."

"That is your choice. Are you willing to pack and take your lunch to school every day then?"

"Yes, if it saves us from having to spend money on lunches."

After this discussion, we tore up the hot lunch request form, and our kids never had a hot lunch again until high school. Once they realized they would be spending their own money instead of spending Mom and Dad's money, their behavior and the choices they made changed— and they became more thoughtful about their decisions. Their decision after only the first day made me think that this program might work better than I ever imagined. My nervousness subsided, and I felt we were on the right path to developing great money athletes.

THE RESULTS

Fast forward to today. Our two oldest kids are now young adults in college. Their financial skills are impressive, and those skills are already changing the course of their future in a positive way with the decisions they are making, including how to fund their education, how they make purchasing decisions, their use of credit, and more. In an unexpected twist, my kids have even taught me how to use certain electronic banking features, such as depositing checks with the use of my smartphone. When that happened, I realized that this program is something powerful for everyone—including the parents who are raising their tweens to be financially fit young adults.

The results you will experience from this program will be difficult to forecast, but I am sure you will be amazed at how well and how quickly your tweens start to pick up the financial concepts they will need later in life. Let me show you how.

THE FOUNDATION

THE LEARNING CHALLENGE

Learning new things is a challenge for anyone. For that reason, regardless of the topic, understanding the process of learning something new and making it "stick" is important.

Following is a chart that represents how most of us experience the learning of new topics. What generally happens is that we experience a spike in our skill level as a result of learning something new. This learning could be the result of taking a class, attending a seminar, reading a book, or even having a conversation with someone who is experienced with a specific topic. However, over time, we start to lose our newfound skill level and return to our starting point, or at least very close to it.

This pattern tends to be true for topics beyond money and finances. For example, consider athletic endeavors such as my golf swing. It always seems that when I take a golf lesson, the coach identifies what is wrong with my swing, helps me change some of the specifics, and gets me to reduce my sliced (not straight) drives off the tee. I certainly end the lesson inspired with this new knowledge and my apparent improved skill level. However, without the coach's periodic guidance, I inevitably return to my old ways and bad habits. I am amazed at how much this pattern exists in sports, business, weight loss, and just about any experience where we are looking for ways to change or improve. Without use and reinforcement, we return to our old, comfortable ways of doing things.

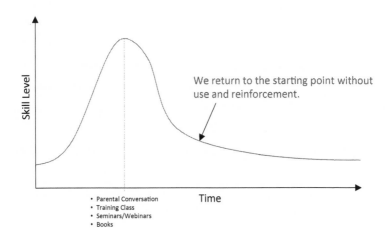

We return to the starting point without use and reinforcement.

Skill Level

Time

- Parental Conversation
- Training Class
- Seminars/Webinars
- Books

Breaking the cycle requires a proactive formula for maintaining and growing the skill level after the initial spike occurs. Additionally, this is where the application of "practice makes you better" comes into play. The next graph reflects this.

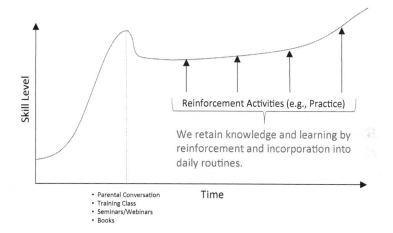

In most cases, the reinforcement activity needed to keep an elevated skill level is consistent practice, whether that's related to improving your golf swing, playing the piano, running, learning a new language, or yes, increasing your financial skills. Developing great skill in something always requires commitment to a level of practice to master the skill and grow it while checking in with the coach or mentor to make sure you are practicing the right way.

THE LEARNING FORMULA

There are many theories and thoughts about how adults and kids learn. I believe the model that best reflects what I experienced with my own kids with regard to learning, as well as the one that seems most relevant based on the feedback I have received from other parents, is the 70:20:10 Model for Learning and Development. This model reflects the way in which optimal real-life learning takes place in that we all learn best by doing.

The 70:20:10 Model for Learning and Development (referred to as the 70:20:10 model) is often credited to the work of Morgan McCall, Robert Eichinger, and Michael Lombardo while working at the Center for Creative Leadership in the 1980s. At that time, they suggested that learning is best achieved when broken down as follows:

- 70 percent dedicated to performing the tasks or activity (doing)
- 20 percent dedicated to coaching and mentoring (feedback and guidance)
- 10 percent dedicated to coursework and training (absorbing)

Although I am sure there are experts who disagree with the details of this model, what I like about it is its simplicity. It's not really important whether 70 percent is correct for the doing or if it is 60 percent or 80 percent. What these percentages say to me is that we all learn best by doing;

therefore, the majority of one's time in learning something new should be dedicated to *doing*.

Coaching and mentoring are also very important, but less so than the doing. Coaching and mentoring provide the "guardrails" to keep the learning process going in the right direction. They provide the feedback loop, so if something gets off track the coach or mentor can bring the action back into alignment.

Lastly, coursework and training provide the initial material content, as well as content related to the evolution of existing content. This can occur through coursework, books, or simply showing a person how to do something for the first time.

Let's use an example of how this formula would work in an activity that many of us have experienced in our lives and one that our sons and daughters usually look forward to: getting a driver's license. I can recall helping all of my kids through this process as they learned to drive. I remember the emotions I felt, including fear.

Although every state has some differences in the process, the general approach to learning to drive is for the beginner to take a series of classes about the rules of the road, the basic protocols on how to drive a car, and the dangers and consequences of making mistakes. Usually what happens next is that the student spends time behind the wheel of a car with an instructor in the passenger seat. The instructor directs the student driver on roads and highways that reinforce the concepts taught within the class. In some cases, there are even special courses set up in parking lots where the students can learn what it feels like to skid on wet pavement. Finally, there is the year that the student drives with a learner's permit to accrue the minimum number of hours needed to practice his or her driving skills.

Allow yourself to ponder this scenario of learning to drive. Although the ratio may not be exact, the coursework probably came close to 10 percent of the time spent "absorbing." The next 20 percent of the time was spent "receiving feedback" from an instructor or parent. Lastly, the bulk of the time spent learning to drive was in actual driving.

Could you even consider allowing your son or daughter to get a driver's license and start driving right after taking the initial class? Of course not! In many cases, however, this is exactly what our kids will be doing when it comes to managing their finances as they grow into young adults. Let's take a look at what the process of learning looks like if we reverse the formula and apply it to how many tweens, teenagers, and young adults learn about money and finances:

- 70 percent dedicated to coursework and training (absorbing)
- 20 percent dedicated to coaching and mentoring (feedback and guidance)
- 10 percent dedicated to performing the tasks or activity (doing)

There are many books, classes, and materials on the market that we have been conditioned to believe will grow our kids' financial responsibility muscle—if our children simply read or participate. We've been led to believe that those resources will provide them the foundation they need. However, just like learning to drive, developing their financial skills will not work if the time spent in actual practice is minimal.

THE ROLE OF PARENTS

Recent studies have shown that only 40 percent of all adults keep some sort of budget and track their spending. Almost 75 percent of families live paycheck to paycheck, and close to 25 percent of families have no money in savings. Young adults increasingly find themselves under more pressure as they try to establish their independence, grow in their careers, and start families—all while being bombarded by the societal pressures to live beyond their means.

Parents play an important role in teaching their kids about finances, but parents can fall short, according to the following information from a 2015 Junior Achievement/ Allstate Foundation Survey:

- Eighty-four percent of teens report looking to their parents for information on how to manage money, but 34 percent of parents say their family's approach to financial matters is to not discuss finances with their children and let kids be kids.

- The number of teens who think their parents don't spend enough time talking to them about managing money has risen significantly (21 percent in 2014 to 32 percent in 2015).

- Millennial parents, ages 18–34, are the least likely to be confident about explaining money management to their kids: 60 percent report feeling confident while 76 percent of parents ages 35–44 and 79 percent of parents ages 45–54 report feeling confident.

These bullet points may catch your attention and make you question your ability to coach or mentor your tween. I certainly had this concern. I am sure every parent has this same fear, and many parents have their own money issues. Affluent parents may want to raise their kids to be financially responsible and not take for granted their family's wealth, yet they may lack the wherewithal to mentor their children toward financial independence.

My parents were not financially savvy, and I found myself learning almost everything on my own. When I became a parent, the fears around money were spinning in my head. As a young adult, I unfortunately did make financial mistakes. For example, when I went to college, like most college students I was bombarded with plenty of credit card offers. I accepted most of them since the companies were very good at giving me something in return. I also did not truly understand during my college years the relationship of credit cards to developing my credit score. In time, I found myself overextended. I even had one debt collector report me to a collection agency.

Those mistakes made during my college years could have been easily avoided if I'd been provided the opportunity to learn about money ahead of time. I simply did not know what

I needed to know to navigate the credit environment. At the time, I was just like Stephanie, and the potential for worse things happening to me financially was certainly possible.

It is true. As a parent, you play an important part in your tween becoming a great money athlete. The journey will have successes and setbacks at times, but having you as a coach, supporter, and guiding force will provide the confidence your tween needs. Just like in any sport, when an athlete has a poor game, event, or competition, the coach is there to help reflect, learn, and plan for how to move forward.

It has been my experience that those parents and families that have made mistakes or had slipups in the past are quite possibly in a better position to coach and mentor their sons and daughters on money than those who have never made a mistake. Bringing forth those experiences that reflect what "not to do" can have a powerful impact on your tween. In my case, teaching my kids the importance of paying bills on time and not procrastinating may prevent them from dealing with a collection agency or taking a hit on their credit score.

Based on my personal experience, I also found that being a trusted adviser and coach to my kids strengthened our overall relationship and allowed us to have more open conversations about other topics, including issues at school, dating, and drugs and alcohol. I believe that being a coach for my kids about money provided a foundation of trust and confidence that carried over into these other areas. Since the area of money and finances is such an important part of life, it makes sense that being a good coach on such an essential life skill will carry over to other life skills. This was certainly a powerful outcome that I had not anticipated.

The Money Athletics Program (for Tweens)

The foundation of this program is based upon your tween learning by experiencing, not just memorizing, the content. With a grasp of the learning challenge, the power of the 70:20:10 model, and your role as the parent and coach, let's dive into what the Money Athletics Program looks like. Similar to developing your tween into an athlete, throughout *Money Athletics* we will touch on multiple focus areas, including the following:

Setting The Playing Field

The first focus item of the Money Athletics Program is to set the field of play. You will define the roles and responsibilities for you and your tween. We will look at the best age to start this program. You will make decisions about where to open bank accounts for your tween, when you will start the program, and when you will end it. You will also define how often you should meet to discuss progress, issues, and concerns. You might think of these meetings as your regular company meetings.

The Baseline Expense Plan

The baseline expense plan gets into the details of the scope of your tween's financial responsibility. This is where it will get interesting, as you will discuss areas such as your tween's clothing, hot lunches at school, birthday gifts for friends, and more. And this plan will cover not only what your tween will be financially responsible for, but also what items you will continue to cover. You will also make decisions about the overall amount of the payment to your tween and its frequency. For example, will you pay your son or daughter once a month, twice a month, or weekly?

The Baseline Future Plan

This part of the Money Athletics Program will discuss the concept of your tweens paying themselves first before paying for any other financial obligations, with directed allocations to various savings accounts. We will also review charitable contributions, the role of chores, and penalty service fees if your tween is not following the rules.

Opening Day—The Rollout

At this point, you will have the definition of your program complete and will be ready to roll it out. We will look at the significance of making opening day a big deal for your tween, and we will consider ideas for how to do that. We will also discuss fun adventure trip ideas to do during this rollout period. This is an exciting part of the program.

You in the role of Coach

Although we have looked at the importance of the role of parents, this section will discuss in more detail their role as coaches. We will review what it takes to be a great coach, not only when things are going well, but what to do when your tween makes mistakes. We will look at the importance of maintaining the long-term goal, that moment when your tween becomes a financially fit young adult.

Strength Training

This part of the program is filled with stories about putting the program into practice. You will gain insight into the things that worked well with our kids as well as some actions that did not.

The intent of the Money Athletics Program is to allow your son or daughter to learn by doing (70 percent), by taking in the feedback and guidance provided through coaching and mentoring (20 percent), and by absorbing the coursework and training (10 percent). Remember, the financial skills that will become your tween's lifelong habits are formed by practicing and starting early so that by the time he or she becomes that young adult, your tween will be ready.

CHAPTER CHECKLIST

✓ Understand the learning challenge, which is that we lose what we don't use.

✓ Understand the core elements of how we all learn, which is mainly by doing (70 percent).

✓ Understand that your role as a mentor or coach is essential to your tween's learning (20 percent).

✓ Understand that teaching and showing your tween how to do something new provides a foundation (10 percent).

✓ Understand the basic road map of the Money Athletics Program.

2

SETTING THE PLAYING FIELD

With a foundational understanding of the program in place, this chapter will guide you through the high-level considerations for creating a program specific to you, your family, and your tween. In other words, you are defining the environment, or the playing field, in which your son or daughter will learn and develop financial skills as part of the Money Athletics Program. You can also download a playbook template from the website MoneyAthletics.com to assist you in capturing the content from this chapter.

AGE TO START

The best age to start this program with your tween is between the ages of eleven and fourteen. To allow for this four-year developmental span of time that typically coincides with late elementary school through middle school, and possibly into a child's first year of high school, I have not followed the traditional dictionary definition of "tween," which includes "a preteen" or a "boy or girl who is eleven or twelve years old." Some children will be ready at eleven or twelve. However, others will show more readiness for this program around the ages of thirteen or fourteen.

A parent's intuition will be an important factor in determining the optimal starting age for each adolescent. For example, my daughter was ready at the early age of eleven. She had the mental capacity to handle the structure of the program and the associated responsibilities. She also had enormous curiosity to learn more about money as well as the structure of the program. Additionally, she was excited to feel more grown-up by doing something that adults do every day. My boys, on the other hand, were more ready at the age of twelve. They did not demonstrate the interest and desire to take on this type of responsibility prior to that age.

There is another reason I believe the ages between eleven and fourteen—those years that represent early adolescence—work well to implement this type of program. Kids in this age range are not yet fully engulfed in the many social and relationship pressures that come into play during their midteens. Additionally, the inevitable need to break away from their reliance on parents—which often looks like rebellion—has probably not yet kicked in either.

Establishing their financial skills early, before all of those teenage distractions become a part of your teens' lives, will provide them a great head start to becoming the independent individuals they will eventually want to become—and in a manner that will be safer and hopefully smoother for everyone. When they begin to experience the pressures to spend money in their later teens or early adult life, they will be in a better position to make those decisions. Whether it's deciding to go out with friends to eat or see a movie, or to buy clothes, or to make other larger purchases, they will be able to make those choices with more ease since they will have been making them for a number of years already.

I wish I could provide you an exact formula for when to start, but in almost every conversation I have had with parents who implemented this program, it came down to parental intuition. Thinking about the following scenarios will help reveal your "gut knowledge" related to their readiness.

1. Does your son or daughter consistently want to buy things from stores, iTunes, and the Internet? An answer of yes to this question could mean your tween is ready.

2. Is your son or daughter knowledgeable about money already, maybe because you have been providing an allowance and teaching some of the financial basics? If yes, this may be a good indicator that your tween is ready. If the answer is no, you may find that he or she is still ready, but you will most likely need to spend more time teaching the financial basics, like balancing an account, as well as the concept of interest since interest will be deposited to their accounts.

3. With regard to nonmonetary readiness factors, do you believe that your tweens have the mental capacity for this responsibility? For instance, do they do their chores without continual reminders or potential consequences? Do they do their homework without the need for you to be on their case to get it done? What other types of responsibilities do they manage within and outside of your home?

Responses to questions such as these will reveal their willingness, readiness, and previous experience with handling responsibility. However, what do you do if the answers are not clear and definitive? Remember, we are discussing the correct age to start this program, not whether you *should* start. For that reason, if you clearly do not feel your son or daughter is ready, then wait six months and reevaluate. If you are on the fence, I suggest you move forward and implement the program because the benefits will far outweigh the risks.

Should you begin the program and discover that it might have been better to wait a little longer, I don't suggest that you stop and then start at a later date. That could lead to your child feeling failure in some way. Instead, I believe it will require a little extra handholding and maybe a decision to break down the responsibilities into even smaller, more bite-sized pieces. Once you see that your child is ready to manage more responsibility and take on a deeper level of ownership, you can pick up the pace and back away a bit more.

I stated earlier that my daughter was ready for the program at eleven. Truthfully, I only realized she was ready in retrospect, after I implemented it simultaneously with her and her older brother. Like most dads, I remember looking at my eleven-year-old daughter and seeing a little girl who was so small and too young to worry about money. I am glad I ultimately listened to my gut and moved forward with her in the program at the same time as my older son. It turned out that she was more than ready and a quick learner.

To summarize, I do believe a parent's intuition is powerful as it relates to our children. The questions and the thought processes described in this section will trigger a gut feel for you related to your son's or daughter's readiness. If you are on the fence, I believe you should lean toward deciding that your tween is ready.

BANK OR CREDIT UNION FOR ACCOUNTS

Setting up accounts with a bank or credit union is essential to this program. The main reason is that banks and credit unions provide the means to track, manage, and carry out banking activities electronically, including through their websites and applications on tablets and smartphones. Using a bank or credit union will offer your tween the ability to manage his or her finances in our modern, electronic age while still allowing for the ability to use cash if and when necessary.

You will need to identify the specific bank or credit union in which to open accounts for your tween. Ideally, it will be the same financial institution where you already do your banking, mainly because of the flexibility it gives you with fund transfers between accounts. However, the main criteria of the bank or credit union you choose should include the following:

- Allows savings accounts for children ten years or older. Most institutions will support this.

- Allows checking accounts for children between the ages of eleven and fourteen. This is one criterion you need to verify. Many banks and credit unions require a minimum age of sixteen to open a checking account.

- Offers a debit card (preferably Visa or Mastercard) to be attached to a tween's checking account. In addition to using this card to purchase items, the tween can usually use it as an ATM card for making deposits and withdrawing cash as well. Like the checking account, this may require a minimum age, so be sure to check with the institution.

- Offers the ability to do online banking. This criterion should include online account review and the ability to pay bills via bill pay and to make account transfers. In actuality, the more features that are available, the better.

- Offers the availability of a mobile app for a smartphone. You will want your tween to have the option to check balances and do certain transactions from a smartphone. This is important since the trends for banking are moving toward the use of banking via our smartphones and tablets. For example, it is now possible to take a picture of a check and deposit it directly through a smartphone app. You are no longer required to go to the bank or ATM to make a deposit. Although this may still be uncomfortable for you, I can almost guarantee that it will not be an issue for your tween.

As the parent, you will need to cosign for all of your tween's accounts. The real benefit for you is that as a co-owner of the accounts, you will be able to monitor the transaction activity that is taking place for each account. One of the benefits to setting up your tween's account at the same institution where you bank is that your login access will allow you to not only see your accounts online, but you will automatically see your son's or daughter's accounts as well.

One other area to keep in mind relates to bank policies. They can change. We learned this lesson at the time I attempted to set up my younger son's accounts. Although the bank I had used for our family's program matched all of the above criteria with my first two children, I ultimately ran into a problem when it was time to create his accounts.

In 2006, I initially set up a savings account and a checking account for each of my two older kids at the same bank where I had been banking for years. I did not have any issues setting up any of the accounts or obtaining debit cards at that time because their age-limit restriction stated that a child had to be ten years of age or older. However, four years later, when I went into the same bank to set up the same types of accounts for my younger son, Tyler, I ran into a challenge. The great recession had hit between the years 2006 and 2010, and apparently my bank had made a change in its policy—one that I didn't know about.

On the day I took Tyler into the bank to set up his accounts, I went up to the teller and stated that I wanted to open checking and savings accounts for him.

"Sorry, sir," she replied, "but your son needs to be at least sixteen years old to open a checking account."

"Really?" I responded. "Can I talk to your manager?"

The young teller proceeded to tell her manager, and that manager came up to me and repeated the same policy about not allowing kids younger than sixteen to open a checking account or be issued a Visa debit card associated with it.

"Can I talk to your manager then?" I asked again.

This time I was told that I would need to speak with the bank's area vice president. I obtained his phone number and called him later that same day. In the meantime, my son was devastated that he was not going to be able to join the family company and start managing his own money—something he was very much looking forward to doing.

I called John, the vice president of the bank, and could tell immediately that he was going to be staunch about the bank's policy. I had not told anybody at the bank that my other kids had been assigned accounts from the ages of eleven and twelve because, quite honestly, I was worried the bank might revoke them.

"John," I asked preemptively, "you are probably thinking to yourself that a parent coming into your bank to open several accounts with an attached Visa debit card represents an example of the irresponsible behavior that has brought our country into the recession we are currently experiencing."

Even though I could not see John's face, I could tell through his responses on the phone that he indeed agreed with that statement. I proceeded to follow my statement by saying, "and if you are thinking that, you would be completely wrong. Here is why." I then gave John the three-minute overview of the Money Athletics Program and told him that I was in fact teaching my kids to be financially responsible kids who will one day grow into great young adults who are wise with their money.

After a brief pause, John responded, "That is brilliant!" He explained that he could not change the policy but would confer with the bank board about making an exception. John ended with, "I will call you tomorrow, as I already have a meeting scheduled with the bank board."

I was certain I would never hear from John again and had already begun to figure out a plan B for Tyler, as well as what I might have to do with my other kids since my daughter was still under the age of sixteen. Although Tyler was disappointed, I assured him that we would figure this out.

To my surprise, John called me the next day. "Craig, we are not able to change the policy of the bank, but you are granted an exception, so you are free to go into the bank and set up the accounts for Tyler. Again, I am impressed with what you are doing. Good luck!"

Wow! What a relief! I had challenged the bank and won. That kind of stuff never happens. When I told Tyler what the bank board had decided, I could see his eyes light up with excitement.

In addition to emphasizing the need to be aware of your bank's policies, especially when it comes to checking accounts and debit cards, I tell this story to let you know that this program and what you are about to do with your tween goes against what many people, and even banks, believe about young people and money. Most believe that irresponsibility and young age go together. Not true! You will likely see evidence of this assumption directed at you and your tween at some point during this program, but I assure you, the people who may challenge you or your tween will ultimately stop and think, like John did, that what you are doing is brilliant.

For example, when my daughter was eleven years old, we went into a store so she could buy a swimsuit since she'd outgrown her current suit. As we proceeded to the checkout register, I was behind her with a shopping cart filled with things I needed to buy. When it was my daughter's turn to make her purchase, she confidently swiped her debit card, signed the electronic pad, and waited for the receipt from the cashier. Throughout this transaction, I could see the puzzled look on the cashier's face. She even looked around for a moment, apparently wondering if my daughter was with a parent. I acknowledged that she was my daughter when the cashier looked my way. Since I was next in line after my daughter, the cashier asked me how old she was and commented that she seemed young to have a Visa debit card. I told her that she was eleven and was learning how to manage her own finances and money. The cashier responded with a smile and commented that she was an impressive young lady. The smile on my daughter's face was priceless.

Accounts You'll Set Up

I know many parents who used piggy banks, jars, or even envelopes to help their kids separate how their money should be used. One of the most common setups I have seen for younger kids teaches them to have a "spending" fund, a "savings" fund, and a "charity" fund. For the program you are creating, the accounts you will set up for your tween should be thought of in much the same way, except that an actual bank will be keeping track of the amounts in the various "piggy banks" you create.

Let's take a look at the accounts you will set up when you first begin this program. Keep in mind that in the beginning you don't have to open every account listed below. As highlighted below, there are only a few accounts that are absolutely necessary for you to begin—one checking account with a debit card tied to it, one savings account, and another savings account to serve as an injury prevention (emergency) account. The concepts behind the optional accounts will be discussed in later chapters. The following should provide some guidance for you to decide if you want to establish any optional accounts initially:

1. **Checking account (must)**—This is a must-have account since this is where the majority of the spending transactions will occur.

2. **Visa/Mastercard debit card (must)**—This is also a must-have and should be attached to your tween's checking account.

3. **Savings account #1 (must)**—This must-have account will serve as your tween's long-term savings account.

4. **Savings account #2 (must)**—This must-have account will serve as your tween's injury prevention (safety net). The injury prevention account is for emergencies and is intended to prevent injuries to your tween's

overall financial plan. If used, the money removed should be replenished.

5. **Savings account #3 for charity (optional)**—We will discuss this in a later chapter, but having a savings account where your tween can deposit and withdraw funds and direct them toward a charity will raise their awareness about the needs of others around them. It is easy for tweens to become self-centered, but with a charitable aspect to their lives, they can develop empathetic views that can result in respect and appreciation for what they have. The reason this account is optional is that you and your family may decide charity is not important to you. However, I would encourage you to do this because of the character-building growth your tween will experience by helping others.

6. **Savings account #4 for special long-term items, such as a car, trip, or other big-ticket item (optional)**— If you believe that your tween will want to save for something like a car, a trip, or an item that has a hefty price tag attached, then this is the account to set up for that reason. You may want to consider this as an account you might want to open later.

7. **Investment/college savings account (optional)**— Many parents do not use a bank savings account to save for college, but this could be a good option to start at this time. We opened college 529 savings plans through which we could receive tax benefits for saving. Some parents even open investment accounts

with a brokerage firm. This account will be discussed in the next chapter and will help to teach your tween about longer-term savings and the concepts around a 401(k) plan, where you can match a percentage that they save. Even if your son or daughter does not go to college, this account will still be important to teach about saving for the long-term.

To wrap up this section related to accounts, I want to mention that your tweens should have an email account as well. This will allow them to receive statements and notices electronically. If they do not already have an email account, you can set up an account via Gmail, Yahoo mail, or another free email option on the web.

PROGRAM REVIEW MEETINGS

As was mentioned in chapter 1, it is important to provide consistent feedback to keep your tween on track, to answer questions, and to monitor progress. There will undoubtedly be many times when your tween will ask questions and consult with you about a particular situation. However, it is important to set aside a consistent time when you can review your tween's progress and answer questions.

I believe the best frequency for this is on a monthly basis, generally at the beginning of the month when your monthly statements become available from the bank. This is the time when you can help your tweens balance their checking and savings accounts. This is also the opportunity to see how they are progressing with savings goals, identify any challenges that have occurred, and review any fees they might have been charged.

This is also a great opportunity for you and your tween to bond over a common activity. Since you perform this same activity with your finances, working with your tween on his or her own financial matters can prove to be a powerful exercise that you engage in together. It reinforces that what your tween is doing is a grown-up activity and that you, as a parent, care about and want to demonstrate how to do it correctly. These financial conversations will help develop a trusting relationship with you. Most likely, your tween will make some mistakes along the way, such as simple adding and subtracting errors, or discover a situation where the debit card was used for more than was in the checking account. Your role will be to coach and guide your tween through these learning opportunities. Not only will this build trust in your ability to be a mentor without imposing additional consequences, but it will also increase his or her financial confidence, which will grow before your eyes.

ISSUE RESOLUTION PROCESS

Any good program would be incomplete without a plan for how to resolve issues that arise during the life of the program. I guarantee some will. Because you cannot forecast everything that might occur, what you want to have in place is a process for resolving issues as they occur. The process should be simple so that when an issue arises, either you or your tween can bring up the need for a conversation and the matter can be discussed in a safe manner in order to reach an agreeable solution.

The way I kept the process simple was by using our monthly review meeting as the time to discuss any issue that surfaced. However, if something could not wait for that meeting, then one would simply let the other know that we needed to talk about an issue. Anyone could bring up the need to have a discussion at any time. Interestingly, as a result of the trust we developed through the program and our process for managing issues when they were younger, now that my kids are older and well versed at managing their own finances, they still call me or sometimes send a simple text message with questions about money.

An example of an issue we dealt with during one of our monthly meetings related to my younger son. I noticed that he was spending a lot of his money on downloadable games for his smartphone. For example, one month he spent close to seventy dollars. Although, to some degree, I needed to allow him to do that, in my opinion, he was spending far more than I thought was appropriate. My concern was that he was ignoring the more important things he was financially responsible for, such as clothing, gifts, and activities with friends. The money he was spending on games was not leaving him with adequate funds to pay for those other items.

At our next meeting, I raised my concern with him. We discussed the issue, including why I thought it was a matter to address and what consequences might occur if he continued spending in that way. We came to an agreement that he could continue to spend his money on the downloadable games, but with a limit of ten dollars per month. That conversation had an immediate impact and almost eliminated the behavior overnight.

As the parent, you will want to monitor your tween's spending habits and bring up issues that can lead to financial challenges. In most cases, I found that the challenges related to their overspending on particular items, such as clothes, games, going out to eat, and other forms of entertainment. As tweens, they were not always able to project how their spending habits would impact agreed-upon financial responsibilities. Those "mistakes" led to wiser decisions over time. Remember that, although you want to assist them in anticipating potential outcomes, you also need to give them leeway to make mistakes and spend foolishly at times. That is how they will learn.

THE ROLE OF CHORES

The role of household chores is quite possibly the question I am asked about most often in relation to this program. My point of view with regard to this program is to help your tweens grow into financially fit young adults, not to make them do chores. That being said, I certainly see the dilemma.

In our family, we took the stance that everyone was required to do certain chores as a member of the family. We all shared in those responsibilities, and nobody could escape from helping out. Those responsibilities started for our kids at a young age, so they were used to what was expected from them long before we implemented the Money Athletics Program. However, our kids did go through a phase around fifteen and sixteen years old when getting them to do their chores became a constant challenge. We began to apply a "service fee" when we were not able to correct a behavior related to a particular chore.

For example, there came a time when my son stopped taking out the garbage and he would not do it without constant nagging. As a result, we applied a service fee of five dollars for each week that he did not take out the garbage at all. When he became too willing to pay the service fee (rather than do the assigned chore), we increased the fee. It only took a few weeks for his behavior to change.

Since I was a co-owner on his account, I was able to transfer the service fee out of his account immediately. Using the service fee approach helped correct the course for any issues we encountered with our tweens' completion of assigned chores. If you feel you may have issues with the completion of chores by your tween, the service fee approach can be an effective way to help resolve it.

As a word of caution, I have seen some parents take the service fee concept overboard by applying a service fee to too many things, including chores, not doing their homework, or after arguments resulting from disagreement between parents and tweens. Imposing service fees should be used sparingly, as going overboard will result in the Money Athletics Program being used as a punishment (taking money away), when it is really meant to serve as a privilege for your tween and a means to help him or her learn how to manage money now and in the future.

MONEY ALL-STARS

As your child grows further into the teenage years and enters high school, there will be additional matters that begin to surface. Those topics, and how I helped my kids navigate them, are the inspiration for the next book in the Moneyletics MAP Series, *Money All-Stars: Your Game Plan to a Financially Fit Teenager*. In that book, we build upon all of the foundational elements outlined in this book. Some of the additional topics discussed in *Money All-Stars* include loans, paying for college, credit scores, and protecting from identity theft. If your tweens are doing well with the concepts in this book by the time they reach the age of fifteen, then adding in those additional topics to their program will serve them well. It will help them grow from a money athlete into a money all-star!

CHAPTER CHECKLIST

✓ Identify the starting age of the program for your tween.

✓ Identify the bank or credit union with which you will set up the program. If possible, use the institution where you currently bank.

✓ Make a list of the accounts you will want to set up and the bank, credit union, or investment company with which you will work.

✓ Set up an email account for your tween if he or she does not already have one.

✓ Determine the frequency and regular meeting dates and times for your program review meetings throughout the program.

✓ Implement a simple issue-resolution process:
a) Either parent or tween can raise an issue
b) Discuss both perspectives in a safe manner
c) Mutually agree on a resolution.

✓ Identify the service fee and the circumstances under which that service fee will be applied.

3

THE BASELINE EXPENSE PLAN

N ow that we have the foundational components of the program ironed out, let's dive into the details of the baseline expense plan you'll create for your tween. In this chapter, we will begin to determine the baseline amount and interval of the paycheck you will provide to your tween. In order to come up with that baseline figure, we will take a look at specific categories of expenses that your tween can be responsible for managing. In the next chapter, we will add to this baseline amount by considering additional "future" categories you may choose to include, such as savings and charitable donations.

The best way to identify the baseline expense plan is to start with a simple list that can be created on a single sheet of paper. At the top of the page, write "The Baseline Expense List." You can also download this form from the MoneyAthletics.com website.

THE BASELINE EXPENSE LIST

The Baseline Expense List will capture the items that you believe are appropriate expenses for your tween to manage and will ultimately become the foundation for the paycheck you will provide. To help get you started, below is the list that I initially used with my older son and daughter. This list is relatively short, which is on purpose. I believe that if you make the list too detailed and too long, it will be more difficult to explain to your son or daughter when you roll out the program. It will also be more complicated to manage.

Item	Annual Cost
Allowance and entertainment ($5/week)	$260
Clothing and shoes	$600
Birthday party gifts to friends	$140
Hot lunches at school	$180
School supplies	$80
Total annual expenses	$1,260

Sample Baseline Expense List

This sample list is not only the Baseline Expense List that I used for all my kids, but it also represents what the majority of other parents I have worked with used as a baseline when they rolled out this program to their tweens. I believe these categories represent the *must be included* items to get you and your tween started. This list includes items that you may provide on a weekly basis, such as hot lunches at school, but the majority of categories represent items that you buy yearly but don't necessarily buy each month.

Let me explain why the categories listed represent a good starting point. Let's take a look at each one separately.

Allowance and entertainment—We paid our kids an allowance each week based upon their grade level in school. Since my daughter was in fifth grade when we rolled out the program, she received five dollars a week. My son was in sixth grade and received six dollars a week. Like many kids, they spent this money on hobbies, treats, songs from iTunes, and souvenirs when we went on a trip somewhere. If you are already paying your tweens an allowance, that amount should absolutely be accounted for here. If you are not paying them an allowance, then I suggest that you allocate an amount similar to what is reflected here to allow your tweens the opportunity to make discretionary purchases on their own.

Clothing and shoes—This item stirs up a lot of conversation with families. Parents wonder whether this category should be on the list and, if so, then what cost amount to allocate. The questions to contemplate vary but include considerations such as the following:

- Have you, as a tween parent, been buying clothes at high-end stores or thrift stores (which will affect the amount to allocate)?

- Do your kids receive clothes from their siblings as hand-me-downs?

- Are they outgrowing their clothes so fast that they need to buy shoes and clothing more frequently?

These are examples of valid concerns to consider in setting the annual cost; however, they are not valid reasons for your tweens not to have to buy their own clothes and shoes.

With regard to my kids, buying their own clothes and shoes provided for some of the best financial-growth learning opportunities that they ever experienced at that age. Purchasing clothes brought up situations to consider, such as whether or not to buy things on sale. They also faced decisions of whether or not to make a purchase based upon the quality of the item. We talked about what makes a piece of clothing higher quality or a pair of shoes sturdy enough to last longer. Those conversations then led into discussions about which particular stores sold quality items and which stores generally sold items that did not last as long.

Although buying clothes that will endure is an important factor to consider, sometimes it doesn't make sense to do so, especially since there is usually a higher price tag associated with such items. Given that many tweens grow at an exceptionally fast rate, it may make better sense to buy lesser-quality (and therefore lesser-priced) clothing items, since your son or daughter may not wear the item for very long. Especially if there is no sibling to hand the clothes down to, a child who is experiencing a growth spurt may be better served by spending less per item on clothing.

You may experience some other unexpected twists along the way as your tween takes responsibility for his or her clothing purchases. For instance, my older son was doing great at managing his money, including how he bought clothes. There came a time, though, when the shoes he was wearing to school had so many holes in them that I could see his toes. The sight of his shoes embarrassed me as a parent. My son's response, when I asked him if he was going to buy shoes anytime soon, was simply this: "I will, but I don't want to spend the money right now." Although I could appreciate his frugalness and his desire to get the most out of his shoes, I did successfully nudge him into buying new shoes the following weekend. For me, the need for proper attire outweighed frugality. Coaching him to see the importance of replacing his worn-out shoes also helped me avoid further embarrassment. I never experienced this particular scenario with my daughter since she never would have been caught dead in shoes that were worn out.

For the most part, it was entertaining to see these types of differences between my sons and daughter, and it also provided me insight into each of their financial personalities as they began to develop. Over time, I was able to anticipate what items each of my kids felt were important.

Birthday Party Gifts for Friends—Throughout the year, our kids were invited to various birthday parties for their friends. These events required them to bring a gift. The way we determined how much to allocate was to simply estimate the number of parties per year and then multiply that number by the average cost of the gift.

Don't worry about estimating perfectly. The goal is to come close. If you think your tween will attend six or seven parties throughout the year, go with the higher number of seven. If, on average, your tween spends twenty dollars on a gift and goes to five parties a year, then set the total amount at one hundred dollars. If you believe the amount will fluctuate from year to year, go with what you believe the higher amount will be. It will be difficult to reduce the amount you are providing for your tween, much like adults don't like to receive a cut in pay, so allocate an amount high enough to cover the higher end of the spectrum.

When your tweens know that they are responsible for the gift, they will be more invested in what they choose and what it costs. Interestingly, we found that all of our kids spent more on gifts for their very best friends than they did for kids they didn't know as well.

If your tweens do not spend the entire allocated amount for gifts, that will be to their benefit. My daughter saved money on gifts for her friends periodically by making a gift instead of buying one. I recall a time when she made a fleece blanket with material we had left over from another project. It was a perfect gift for her friend, and she saved the money for herself.

Hot lunches at school—The school our kids attended offered hot lunches, and we paid roughly twenty dollars a month for the nine months they were in school each year. I thought this was a great item to have on the list since it would require our kids to be involved in what meals they would select and their associated cost. As I mentioned in the introduction, the irony was that once we rolled out the program, our kids stopped eating hot lunches and took their lunch to school every day. At the time, I did not see that coming.

This is an item that may not appear on your tweens' lists, either because their school doesn't offer hot lunches or because they already prefer to bring their own lunch to school. I invite you to consider those items you purchase for your tween regularly, such as a magazine subscription for kids, events at an American Girl store, or a weekly entrance fee to a recreation center. As you consider an item, think about the process your son or daughter will go through to regularly make the purchase and determine if it possesses a significant financial learning opportunity.

School supplies—The category of school supplies represents items that your tween will mostly buy at the beginning of the school year. As the school year progresses, some items will need to be replenished. This means that in late summer of every year, your tween will need to have enough money in the checking account to buy supplies for the upcoming school year as well as reserve some money to replace those items that run out during the course of the year. This seemed to surprise my kids every year and provided the foundation for a great conversation about planning and budgeting.

Just as those of us who receive a paycheck understand that we receive the same paycheck each month, regardless of the additional expenses we may have in any given month, our tweens have the opportunity to begin to understand that they must look ahead to those fluctuations in their own expenditures. The "extra money" we see in our account may not actually be extra when we consider the expenses coming along further down the road.

◎ ◎ ◎

As explained earlier in this chapter, the above categories represent a solid foundation for a Baseline Expense List and are what I used for my tweens. If there are other categories to include for your tween, feel free to expand your list to accommodate your son's or daughter's individual needs. Be sure those categories represent items you pay for regularly on behalf of your son or daughter because then they will also offer an opportunity to teach your tween more financial responsibility.

Lastly, you should expect that the categories on this list may evolve as your son or daughter grows older—during the latter years of elementary school and after a move into middle school. There may be various after-school activities, such as chess club, theatrical plays, sports activities, or math club. Their interests may take them into other hobbies as they grow older. As the parent, you will need to decide if you want to expand your son's or daughter's item list, with associated costs, or cover the expenses yourself.

As you complete your Baseline Expense List, be careful about allocating too much of an annual cost to an item. Rather, strive to determine a realistic amount for what your son or daughter is likely to spend on the item. Be sure that you do not incorporate into the initial line items future expense increases, such as amounts to cover for the probability that clothing will become costlier when your son or daughter goes to middle school. During their tween years, they will already feel inspired and empowered by the program regardless of the amount allocated to an item. You can make annual adjustments if necessary, especially if costs for items go up. This can then be presented as a raise to your tween.

Another reason to keep the annual cost amount reasonable, and one that I found to be extremely important for our family, is that by keeping the total cost amount limited, you set the stage for your tweens to want to get a job when they get older. My daughter began babysitting for parents in the neighborhood starting at the age of twelve, so she quickly started to supplement the salary we were providing through this program. That was good for her on many fronts. Her confidence, by having a job that paid her money, gave her a sense of responsibility and accountability as well as the additional financial reward. That was important for my daughter, as she developed a desire to spend more money on clothes when she was in middle school.

We did evaluate the amounts for each line item every year and provided our children a "raise" based upon our findings. For my kids, the amount was generally about $10 each time we gave a raise. The costs for these items went up even higher as they entered high school; however, at that point, we kept the annual cost amount for the various line items the same. By doing so, the incentive for them to obtain a job increased so they could raise their income.

There will be no incentive for your children to work if they have ample money coming in and if you continually increase the amount each year. Even if your son or daughter does not plan to have a job in high school, it is still important to keep these budgets practical and not provide them with too much money. Having a realistic limit is a major contributor to their financial learning.

SETTING THE BASELINE PAYCHECK AMOUNT

Now that you have a list of items your tween will be responsible for and have determined their associated annual cost, you can calculate the base amount of your tween's paycheck.

First, add up the total amount for all items on the list. In my example list, the total amount equals $1,260 annually. Next, determine the payment interval for paying your son or daughter. Monthly is a good interval, but if you receive a paycheck every two weeks, or twice a month, you may want to have your tween receive a paycheck according to that same schedule.

If you decide to pay your tween monthly, your yearly payments will total twelve. If you pay twice a month, they'll total twenty-four, and if you pay every two weeks, they'll total twenty-six. With the annual cost and the interval determined, you can now calculate the amount of a baseline paycheck. Using my example, $1,260 divided by twelve payments a year results in a paycheck amount of $105 per month.

This is a big milestone to have achieved; however, the final paycheck amount is not completely calculated just yet. As I mentioned at the beginning of this chapter, the next chapter will take us into the various additional "future" allocations—such as savings accounts and charity—that you will consider and potentially add to this amount. At this point, however, give yourself a pat on the back for all the hard work you have already accomplished.

Before we proceed to the next chapter, there are a few other topics to address. These items represent hot buttons for many parents, so rather than avoid them or address them down the road, let's take a look at them as part of baseline expense considerations.

WHAT ABOUT SMARTPHONES?

The smartphone conversation comes up with almost every family I talk to about the Money Athletics Program. By the time our children become tweens, most have a smartphone. In some ways, providing a smartphone for your tween is easier now than in the past, since the smartphone service providers understand that younger kids are key customers for their service. Most, if not all, providers have added unlimited plans as well as family plans. I am not advocating that your son or daughter have a smartphone, but I do think it is important to provide some guidelines around one if they do.

What we did for our kids, and why we did not include this on the Baseline Expense List, is that we covered the initial cost of each smartphone, two years of insurance on the phone, and the monthly service charges. Our children were responsible for any overages beyond the base plan. For instance, if they used too much data or sent too many text messages, they were responsible for paying that overage amount. They were also responsible for replacing a phone if they lost or damaged it. That amount could range from about

$100 to pay for the deductible on a damaged phone to the full cost of a phone if they lost it, since the phone insurance plan covers damage but not loss. This specific discussion helped support the reason for them to maintain an injury prevention savings account, which we will discuss in the next chapter. That savings was there to provide access to money in the event of an emergency.

For instance, not long after we rolled out this program to our kids, my daughter broke the screen on her smartphone, but the phone still worked. She had some money in her injury prevention account but not the full amount to cover the deductible cost to replace her phone, so she went almost two months using a phone with a spider web of cracks on the screen. Once she had the money to repair the phone, not only did she have it repaired, but she also bought a protective case.

An interesting side effect of my daughter being the first to experience this issue was the impact it had on her brothers. Both boys remembered the relative pain she went through having to deal with a phone that was not perfect. She complained a lot at first, but when she realized that Mom and Dad were not going to budge, she stopped. All of my kids realized the importance of taking care of their phones as a result of her dilemma.

EXTRA PROJECTS

In the last chapter, we discussed regular household chores. I shared that I was not a fan of paying our kids for those chores. However, there were a number of activities

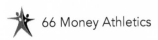

and projects for which we did pay our kids extra. Most of those items fell outside what we called normal household chores.

For example, we paid our older son each time he mowed the lawn. We also paid our kids to shovel snow from the driveway and sidewalk after a storm. When our older kids were at the age that they could babysit their younger sibling, we paid them for that. We also had other projects that were worthwhile to pay them for when those special projects arose. Examples of such projects included staining the fence or helping to paint a room in the house. Those activities went beyond normal household chores, such as keeping their rooms clean, taking out the trash, unloading the dishwasher, etc. Providing special opportunities for extra projects is a way to allow your tween to make additional income.

It's OK for Parents to Treat, But Be Cautious

Although we are in the process of working through the scope of your tween's financial responsibility, keep in mind that they should not be held responsible for the items on the Baseline Expense List at all times. You, as the parent, should still feel empowered to provide things for your son or daughter without them having to pay for it. In other words, there need to be times when Mom or Dad is treating. For example, if we went to the movies as a family, or out to eat as a family, we treated everyone to the event. If we went out for ice cream as a family, it was our treat. I also had regular one-on-one dates with our kids, and those were my treat as well. My point is that you should still feel honored to provide for your tween. Not only is it an honor for you, but it creates a special occasion for your tween.

The word of caution applies when your son or daughter starts to get wise to the circumstances under which you offer to pay and then invites you along to certain events, intending for you to pay for those occasions. All of my kids became quite skilled at inviting me to go out for ice cream, to hit golf balls at the driving range, or even to go with them to the movies. Being the "softy" that I can be, I will say that it worked quite well, since I love to spend time with my kids.

However, there were times when they would test me by inviting me along with the clear motivation to get me to buy something for them. For instance, they might try to convince me that a song on iTunes was a great song that they thought I would like and, therefore, should buy. As the parent, your tweens will undoubtedly test you to pay for things on their behalf. Many times I responded, "Honey, you have money of your own if that is important to you."

The key takeaway I want to leave with you from this section is that although you are rolling out a great program that has structure and will help your tween develop great financial skills, don't be too rigid with it. Allow yourself to enjoy parenthood and to cherish time with your kids without money and your family's financial program always getting in the way.

CHAPTER CHECKLIST

✓ Identify the items for your Baseline Expense List that will aid in setting a base salary amount.

✓ Provide an annual target cost for the items on the Baseline Expense List.

✓ Identify the interval you plan to use to pay your tween and determine the baseline paycheck amount.

✓ If your son or daughter will have a smartphone, create and assign the financial responsibilities for the phone and service plan.

✓ Identify the extra projects and activities where extra money can be earned as well as what you will pay.

✓ Recognize that your son or daughter may test you and attempt to have you pay for items for which they should be responsible to pay.

✓ Don't be too rigid with this program by making everything about the money and finances.

✓ It is OK to be a "softy" at times. You are still the parent.

4

THE BASELINE FUTURE PLAN

Congratulations, you have completed the baseline expense planning part of the Money Athletics Program, where we covered expenses that your tween will be responsible for managing. In this chapter, we will build upon that baseline by considering categories that go beyond expenses and serve to prepare your tweens for their future. These categories offer the opportunity to grow their understanding and skills, which will propel them to a level of financial freedom most young adults struggle with today.

In general, many people struggle financially, living paycheck to paycheck and barely covering their expenses. Most will say that they just can't seem to get ahead. They never have anything left over after paying their expenses. In other words, they pay themselves last. The categories we will consider in this chapter will help your tweens learn valuable practices to pay themselves first and help to prevent them from living paycheck to paycheck when they become young adults.

CONCEPT OF PAY YOURSELF FIRST

Most people wait and only save what's left over at the end of the pay period—which oftentimes, or most times, equates to zero. That represents paying themselves last. Their experience is such that by the time they've paid for their expenses, which include housing, groceries, utilities, and maybe some indulgences like dinners out at a restaurant, they don't have enough left to add to savings or give to charity. With each paycheck, they may have the intention to put aside some money, but each pay period yields the same result—there's nothing left once they've met all their monthly obligations. And so the cycle goes and goes.

Paying yourself first means that you make allocations to accounts that will benefit you in the future—before you pay for anything that is required to meet your present obligations and needs. Paying yourself first takes a long time to develop into a habit, largely because there isn't immediate gratification for doing so. This can be even more challenging for your tween since most kids at this age are not thinking about their future or long-term goals. However, during your son's or daughter's tween years, you will most likely begin to hear comments like "when I go to college," "when I move out of the house," "when I get my own car," and other statements that indicate future aspirations. These comments will continue to expand as your tweens enter their teen years and can create wonderful moments that can lead to great conversations with them.

In a later chapter, we will look at how you can turn these conversations into fun exploratory exercises. For now, allow them to dream and do not squash their thoughts with a comment like "That type of house will be way too expensive for you," or "You won't be able to afford a car like that." It will certainly be tempting to think that way with regard to your son or daughter. I know I did. But restrain yourself.

Because your tweens are mainly accustomed to living in the moment, with little focus on the future, do not take that as a reason to not introduce the accounts we will consider in this chapter. I believe you should move forward with them even if your tweens do not yet understand their value. When they do begin to understand the concepts behind each of these accounts, they will be pleased that you helped them start.

For example, we started with many of the accounts you will read about in the following pages when we initially rolled out the Money Athletics Program. As a result, these various accounts were being funded from an early age.

Returning to the example from the previous chapter, when my daughter broke the screen on her smartphone and did not have enough money in her checking account to pay for it, she had some money in her injury prevention account—an account we'll be looking at in just a moment. However, she needed a couple of more months of deposits to fix her phone. She was so glad that she had that money already set aside, even though she had not understood the value of this account when we first set it up. From that point on, she understood.

So, whether or not your tweens are already thinking about the future, the Money Athletics Program will help them develop those skills. Let's take a look at the various types of accounts you may consider for your tweens and how you will decide which allocations to include.

INJURY PREVENTION ACCOUNT (EMERGENCY FUND)

In the spirit of *Money Athletics*, I like to call the emergency fund the injury prevention account. Developing a habit around having an injury prevention account will probably be one of the best financial habits for your son or daughter to form at an early age. The sole purpose of this account is to provide a safety net when unexpected financial issues arise. Although it is unlikely that your tweens will experience financial issues at their young age, they will certainly experience financial events as they grow older. Starting an injury prevention account early will have them appreciating that they have such an account when situations arise down the road.

For instance, my younger son had to tap into his injury prevention account not long after he received his driver's license because of a moving violation he received when he slid into a neighbor's fence on a snowy day. It is hard to forecast what your son or daughter may financially need in the future, but I assure you your tween will have an event occur when such an account will be appreciated.

This is one allocation that I feel is a "must have" account for your tween. The reason I feel so strongly about starting an injury prevention account is because nearly half the adults in the United States lack any type of financial safety net to access when financial issues arise. You have the ability to help your tween not end up in that category. Your tween can avoid being a part of that statistic by developing the habit of funding an account that will be available should an emergency arise.

Here are three reasons why an injury prevention account is important for your tweens:

1. They will have something to fall back on when an unexpected expense arises. As I previously stated, unexpected expenses do not happen as often for kids in their tween years, but developing the habit for this account as a tween will best prepare them for their future.

2. They will learn that they can avoid going into debt or pulling from other accounts if they are unexpectedly in need of funds. This is important because it is very difficult to return to "paying yourself first" if you have to pay off other financial obligations.

3. They will have peace of mind that if something happens financially to them, they will be prepared for it. Again, at a young age, they may not fully grasp the idea about peace of mind, but because it will become a habit, they will certainly appreciate this concept as they grow older. Both my son and daughter breathed a huge sigh of relief when they were able to pay for

the moving violation ticket and the phone repair themselves without having to ask Mom and Dad to bail them out. And the confidence they displayed was exciting for us to see.

So, how much should be allocated to the injury prevention account? As an adult, most experts state that a person should have around six months or so of expenses contained within such an account. Well, it takes time to fund an account with sufficient money to cover six months of expenses. I believe a good amount to start with is 5 percent. This allows you to keep the overall budget for this program reasonable. If your budget can support a higher number, such as 10 percent, I highly encourage that you raise it to that level since the quicker this account gets funded, the better. Even at that rate, it will take your tween a number of years to accumulate enough money in this account to cover a significant emergency expense.

One note of caution: Do not fund this account yourself! It is important that your children know they are "paying *themselves* first" and funding this account. This is a habit you want them to carry forward into adulthood. They cannot expect you to be their financial insurance when financial emergencies happen to them as adults, and I am certain you do not want to carry that burden as they go forward in life.

Long-Term Savings Accounts

The purpose of a long-term savings account is to save for a long-term goal. Long-term goals can take on many forms for

your tweens. Some of the most common ones include saving for a car that they will purchase when they reach driving age, saving for a trip to a destination that they are passionate about, and hobbies. Hobbies include areas such as music and sports, where items like a new guitar, expensive baseball bat, or golf clubs may be desired but are not absolutely necessary.

The main reason for our kids' long-term savings accounts was to save for their college expenses. They knew from a young age that they wanted to go to college and study for a career that was meaningful to them. We told them that we would help pay for college, but that they would need to cover many college-related expenses themselves. During their tween years, we did not get into a detailed college discussion with our sons or daughter; we simply shared with them that college is expensive and that the sooner they started to save, the better off they would be.

It turned out that during our kids' tween years their goals changed so often it was not possible to specifically plan for their longer-term financial goals beyond their goal to attend college. For example, my younger son stopped liking baseball and started playing lacrosse. My daughter thought she might want a car in high school, but as she got older, she became comfortable sharing the family car and getting a ride to school from her older brother. Also, it turned out that birthday gifts from grandparents and Christmas gifts from Santa fulfilled some of their long-term goals so there was no need to save for them any longer.

If you knew with certainty everything your son or daughter would be saving for in the future, then you could set up savings accounts for each of those goals. However, my experience with our kids helped me understand that keeping it simple is the best approach. Setting up a single savings account that is intended for long-term savings is really all you need for your tween. Because you will likely experience your children changing their long-term goals many times during their tween years, I believe you will appreciate the simplicity of one account.

The next question about the long-term savings account is how much to allocate toward it. There really is no specific formula to apply here, especially since you will not know the specific long-term goals or their associated costs. For this account, we allocated the same amount as we did for the injury prevention account: 10 percent. But even starting with 5 percent for this account is a good place to begin. The exact percentage you choose will depend upon what you consider a comfortable budget for you to maintain in order to fund your son's or daughter's accounts.

Our kids have continued as adults to use their long-term savings account. I have been pleased to see that they grasped the concept of "paying themselves first," which is now a solid part of their financial skills portfolio.

401(K) ACCOUNT

It may surprise you to see that a 401(k) is part of the Money Athletics Program for tweens—maybe you believe it is too complex a subject to introduce to your tween. I had the same concern with my kids when they were eleven and twelve, yet it turned out that this concept and the discussions we had surrounding the 401(k) plan in their tween years are something they remember as adults today. Let me share with you the 401(k) concepts I presented to them.

First, I explained what a 401(k) account is. Without going into the details of the tax code behind it, I simply stated that it is almost the same as the long-term savings account—in that you make deposits into it. The difference is that you cannot take the money out as easily, because the money needs to be used for *very, very* long-term goals. I went on to discuss that many 401(k) plans have a matching contribution component to them.

For the sake of keeping it simple, I explained that for the money they allocated to the 401(k) plan, Mom and Dad would match their deposit dollar-for-dollar. This meant that their contribution would immediately double in size for every deposit they made into it. The benefit of this was that they would be able to reach their goals twice as fast.

For the Money Athletics Program, you will not be setting up an actual 401(k) plan—you will be simply applying the concepts of the 401(k) plan to a separate savings account you set up for your tween. There are multiple options for this account, but generally, I suggest one of the following three:

1. College savings account—The first question to consider is whether you think your tweens have a desire to attend college. This is important since setting up an account, such as a 529 college savings plan, for your tweens locks you into using those funds for their higher education. However, if you are unsure if college is in your son's or daughter's future, there is no reason to use a college savings account for the 401(k).

If, however, you believe your son or daughter will be attending college in the future, then this is a great use for the 401(k) account. In fact, this is what we did for all three of our kids. We felt it was important for them to have "skin" in the game when it came to funding their college education, and this was a great vehicle to teach them about the concepts of the 401(k) and at the same time give them the pride of contributing to their own college education.

If a college savings account is the right option for you, you will need to look into the specific requirements for an account in the state where you reside. Be sure to consult with your tax or financial adviser if you have any questions. I was able to find information about our state's 529 plans through an online search, so doing a search may provide you with all the answers you need.

2. Retirement Account—Retirement account? For a tween? I know this may sound unusual, but if you ponder the benefits of starting an account at such a young age, the positive outcomes can be astounding since your son or daughter would be starting to save for retirement ten to fifteen years before most financial experts recommend they begin. Imagine having that many extra years to contribute to a retirement nest egg.

The specific account that is set up to support this can vary. You can set up a custodial account with a brokerage firm. You can open a certificate of deposit account or savings account, and then when your son or daughter is older, you can migrate that account to an investment account. The options are quite vast.

You can find many retirement calculators on the Internet or via investment company websites. All of them encourage starting early to build a retirement nest egg. However, none of them discusses starting in your tween years. I put together a simple spreadsheet to show my tweens how fast they could grow their retirement funds if they started at their young age and saved just fifteen dollars a month. I have provided a similar one on MoneyAthletics.com for you to download if you wish. I explained to my kids that if I matched dollar-for-dollar, their fifteen dollars would result in a total of thirty dollars a month going into their 401(k). Using basic financial principles and playing with the amount saved each month, the spreadsheet revealed that they could grow their accounts into the hundreds of thousands of dollars, or even millions, by the time they reached the age of sixty-five.

I was also able to show them how powerful it would be to start early and build that type of wealth. This was one of the conversations that was extremely fun to engage in with my kids. Imagine your son or daughter asking, "What if I contributed this much? What if I always contributed Grandma and Grandpa's Christmas money to that account?" We had one conversation on this topic that went for over an hour, with my kids dreaming about becoming wealthy and what they would do with the money. Dreams included a big house, a private jet, a pink Bentley car, and lots of traveling. There were also discussions about helping less fortunate people and kids. I interjected how wonderful it would be for them to take care of their aging parents! That did not go over so well.

Although we chose to use the 401(k) approach for the college savings account instead of the retirement account, looking back I will say that I wish I had taken the retirement account approach and encouraged them to get into a lifelong habit of saving for retirement. Saving for retirement will be a lengthy journey for your children that is likely to continue into their sixties—close to fifty years from their current age. Saving for college, though also important, is a much shorter journey that is probably closer to ten years. If we had begun the retirement account, when they became adults I would have simply migrated that account into some type of investment account where they could continue that long-term savings habit.

Like the other accounts, what is the right amount to allocate to the 401(k) plan account? I did not apply a complex formula to this either and settled on 10 percent, which is the same percentage I always used. Like the previous accounts, 5 percent is also a great starting point. You can always start at 5 percent and raise the percentage higher when your son or daughter reaches high school. Because I started with 10 percent with my kids, they carried that same percentage forward as they started to work for companies that offered formal 401(k) programs.

It is also important to decide on the matching amount you will provide. Keeping it simple, I matched dollar-for-dollar with no cap. I did not run into a problem with not having a cap, but I can foresee that some kids might be aggressive in building their 401(k). As a result, this could place you in a financial pickle if they want to place every Christmas gift or birthday gift of money they receive into their 401(k) account so you will match the contribution. If you foresee that as a possible scenario with any of your children, then place a cap on the amount you'll match—for instance, $500, $1,000, or whatever you feel comfortable with.

3. Down Payment for House/Car—If a college savings account or retirement account is not a fit for your son or daughter, then another good option is to set up a savings account with a focus to save for a down payment on a house or car in the future. You would still apply the matching approach to this account, and you could cap the match amount if you felt it was necessary. The key to this account is that your tweens will not use the money in this account until they are ready to buy their first house or car.

As you can tell, I am a big fan of having the 401(k) account in the allocations part of the Money Athletics Program. The reason is due to the results I am now seeing with my kids. As adults, they understand and participate in the 401(k) plans at their jobs. All three of my kids exceeded my expectations in how well they grasped the 401(k) concepts and the matching benefits. They are making smart decisions today about their own retirements, even in their young twenties. I could never have forecast such a successful outcome when I was looking into their cute eleven- and twelve-year-old faces. Although this is an optional allocation account, I believe your kids will benefit greatly if you implement it with them as tweens.

CHARITY

Giving to charity was a principle we felt was important for our kids to learn and grow from. Because our family has been blessed in so many ways, we've always felt that giving back was a way to express our thanks for our blessings and provide benefit for causes we cared about. Giving to charity is a very personal decision in each family, and for that reason, it may or may not be something you want to have as part of your tween's program.

Like the savings account, the charity account is simply a savings account that is funded with each paycheck. Again, like the other accounts, I believe the amount each month to dedicate to charity should be 5 percent to 10 percent.

As with the previous accounts described, the percentage you assign is up to you and can be more or less. What makes this account somewhat different is that the funds accrued will be directed to charitable causes. The donations could be directed to your church, charitable missions, disease research causes, animal rescue organizations, or any cause or organization your tween decides to support. Over the years, our kids contributed to many of the above categories of charities, as well as many others.

What giving to charity did for our three kids, starting at such a young age, was instill in them that they could make a difference, even on a small scale. It was also not so much the amount they gave to the charity, but the conversations around the causes that created more opportunities for learning. For example, one of my son's friends was diagnosed with leukemia when he was seventeen. It was a very difficult struggle for his friend, and he eventually lost the battle after a year and a half. My son contributed to the family as well as to the Leukemia & Lymphoma Society, and I watched him develop empathy for others that can only be learned through personal experience.

What is interesting about giving to charity is that your heart follows. All three of my kids have donated their time to causes over the years, not because they had to, but because giving to others has become a part of their human fabric. I am convinced that charitable giving has been one of the major influences for my daughter's choice to go into a career in health care so she can help others.

Although this is an optional account, the return you'll receive by making it a part of your Money Athletics Program may be beyond measure with regard to your tween's character development.

BASELINE FUTURE ALLOCATIONS SUMMARY

Now that we have reviewed the various possible allocations in your tween's baseline future plan, let's summarize your accounts and the percentage allocations. There are also downloadable forms on the MoneyAthletics. com website to help you with this.

Account	Percentage Allocation
Injury Prevention	5% to 10%
Long-Term Savings	5% to 10%
401(k)	5% to 10%
Charity	5% to 10%
Total Percentage	20% to 40%

Baseline Future Allocations Table

You now know the percentage amount that you will be allocating on behalf of your tweens, setting the stage so they can learn to "pay themselves first." In the Baseline Future Allocations Table example, I allocated 20 percent to 40 percent of their paycheck to the various accounts listed. As has been discussed in this chapter, you may choose all, some, or none of these accounts, and your percentages may be different from the range I've set out. The beauty of the Money Athletics Program is that you get to choose what is best for you and your tween.

In the next chapter, we will turn your allocated percentages into an actual dollar amount, so you will know exactly how much you will be paying your tween in every paycheck. We almost have all the planning done!

CHAPTER CHECKLIST

✓ Identify the need for an injury prevention account and the percentage to be allocated.

✓ Identify the need and potential basis for a long-term savings account and the percentage to be allocated.

✓ Identify the need and potential basis for a 401(k) account and the percentage to be allocated.

✓ Identify whether a charitable giving account is important for you and your son or daughter and the percentage to be allocated.

✓ Determine the total percentage amount for "pay yourself first" allocations.

5

OPENING DAY-THE ROLLOUT

In the last two chapters, we reviewed the baseline expense plan and the baseline future plan. In this chapter, we are going to bring all of that work together and focus on creating the program and making it ready to roll out to your tween.

The first step is to determine the gross salary you are going to pay your son or daughter. Gross salary is the amount you will pay your tween on a regular basis before any allocations or deductions are subtracted. Having completed the work on expenses and allocations, we will now use that information to determine the gross salary.

Gross Salary

To determine your tween's gross salary, you will take the results from the baseline expense plan you created in chapter 3 and the baseline future plan you created in chapter 4. The combination of the two will determine your tween's gross annual salary. The following sections will walk you through the calculations, but you can also find a simple downloadable spreadsheet on the MoneyAthletics.com website that will do the calculations for you once you enter your information.

A Look at the Kaley Family Example

Before we begin to look at your calculations, let's walk through how I determined our tweens' gross annual salary. My first goal was to fill in the missing fields in the following table.

	Annual Dollar Amount	Percentage of Gross Annual Salary
Total Annual Expenditures	$_____	_____%
Total Annual Allocations	$_____	_____%
Gross Annual Salary	$_____	**100%**

Gross Annual Salary Table

After doing the work outlined in chapters 3 and 4, the results for our children were the following:

Item	Annual Cost
Allowance and Entertainment ($5/week)	$260
Clothing and Shoes	$600
Birthday Party Gifts to Friends	$140
Hot Lunches at School	$180
School Supplies	$80
Total Annual Expenditures	$1,260

Baseline Expense List

Account	Percentage Allocation
Injury Prevention	10%
Long-Term Savings	10%
401(k)	10%
Charity	10%
Total Annual Allocations	40%

Baseline Future Allocations Table

I was immediately able to take the results from each of those tables and fill in two of the unknown fields in the Gross Annual Salary Table, which resulted in the following:

	Annual Dollar Amount	Percentage of Gross Annual Salary
Total Annual Expenditures	$1,260	_____%
Total Annual Allocations	$_____	40%
Gross Annual Salary	$_____	**100%**

Gross Annual Salary Table

The next steps involved a bit more problem solving. I needed to determine the percentage value for the total annual expenditures. The equation to help me determine that was as follows:

Total Annual Expenditures %
+ Total Annual Allocations %
= 100% of Gross Annual Salary

Together, the total annual expenditures percentage and the total annual allocations percentage needed to equal 100 percent. Since I knew the total annual allocations percentage, I subtracted that value (40 percent) from my gross annual salary percentage (100 percent) to arrive at my total annual expenditures percentage (60 percent) and entered that in the table.

	Annual Dollar Amount	Percentage of Gross Annual Salary
Total Annual Expenditures	$1,260	60%
Total Annual Allocations	$_____	40%
Gross Annual Salary	$_____	**100%**

Gross Annual Salary Table

Because I determined both the annual dollar amount and the percentage of gross annual salary for total annual expenditures, I could then determine the gross annual salary with the following equation:

Gross Annual Salary = Total Annual Expenditures dollar amount divided by decimal equivalent of Total Annual Expenditures percentage of gross annual salary:

The resulting equation was:

Gross Annual Salary = $1,260 divided by 0.6

This calculation resulted in the gross annual salary amount of **$2,100.**

Updating the table with this value gave us the following:

	Annual Dollar Amount	Percentage of Gross Annual Salary
Total Annual Expenditures	$1,260	60%
Total Annual Allocations	$_____	40%
Gross Annual Salary	**$2,100**	**100%**

Gross Annual Salary Table

The next step in completing the table was straightforward, using the following equation:

Total Annual Allocations =
Gross Annual Salary – Total Annual Expenditures

To arrive at the total annual allocations, I subtracted the total annual expenditures ($1,260) from the gross annual salary ($2,100) to arrive at $840, which was the last number to complete the table.

	Annual Dollar Amount	Percentage of Gross Annual Salary
Total Annual Expenditures	$1,260	60%
Total Annual Allocations	$840	40%
Gross Annual Salary	**$2,100**	**100%**

Gross Annual Salary Table

The last step in this process was to determine the gross salary of each paycheck since we were not intending to pay our tweens only once a year. If you recall, in chapter 2 we discussed the interval for the paycheck. In our family, we paid our kids monthly, so I took the gross annual salary and divided by 12 to determine the monthly gross salary amount.

$2,100 ÷ 12 = $175 per month

With this $175 amount calculated, I then determined the specific dollar amounts for each paycheck. Referring back to the percentages assigned and entered into the Baseline Future Allocations table, which was 10% for each item, here is what I arrived at for each monthly paycheck:

Gross Monthly Salary	$175.00
Allocation for Injury Prevention (10%)	- $17.50
Allocation for Long-Term Savings (10%)	- $17.50
Allocation for 401(k)* (10%)	- $17.50
Allocation for Charity (10%)	- $17.50
Net Monthly Salary (60%)	$105.00

*Since we matched our tweens' 401(k) accounts, we then added an extra $17.50 per tween each month from our own funds. So the $17.50 from each tween and the $17.50 from us meant total deposits of $35 per month into each 401(k) account.

⊙ ⊙ ⊙

Now it's time to determine the gross annual salary for your tween. We are going to go through the same process for you, using the same tables and structure that I used for my family.

	Annual Dollar Amount	Percentage of Gross Annual Salary
Total Annual Expenditures	$_____	_____%
Total Annual Allocations	$_____	_____%
Gross Annual Salary	**$_____**	**100%**

Your Gross Annual Salary Table

Step 1: The first step is to fill in the Baseline Expense Table. For each line in the Baseline Expense Table, enter the annual cost amount that you determined in chapter 3.

Item	Annual Cost
Allowance and Entertainment	$
Clothing and Shoes	$
Birthday Party Gifts to Friends	$
Hot Lunches at School	$
School Supplies	$
Additional Item #1 (if you have something specific that I did not have)	$

Additional Item #2 (if you have something specific that I did not have)	$
Your Total Annual Expenditures	$

Your Baseline Expense List

Step 2: The second step is to enter the percentages of the Baseline Future Allocations Table. For each line in the Baseline Future Allocations Table, enter the percentage allocation that you determined in chapter 4.

Account	Percentage Allocation
Injury Prevention	%
Long-Term Savings	%
401(k)	%
Charity	%
Your Total Allocations Percentage	%

Your Baseline Future Allocations Table

Step 3: The third step is to update your Gross Annual Salary Table with the values from the previous tables that you now know (the total annual allocations percentage and the total annual expenditures).

	Annual Dollar Amount	Percentage of Gross Annual Salary
Total Annual Expenditures	$_____ (Enter Your Total Annual Expenditures)	_____%
Total Annual Allocations	$_____	_____% (Enter Your Total Allocations Percentage)
Gross Annual Salary	$_____	**100%**

Gross Annual Salary Table

Step 4: In this step, we are going to determine the percentage value for your total annual expenditures. The equation to help us determine that is the following:

Total Annual Expenditures %
+ Total Annual Allocations %
= 100% of Gross Annual Salary

Together, the total allocations percentage and the total annual allocations percentage need to equal 100 percent. Since you now know the total annual allocations percentage and the fact that the total of the two values equals 100 percent, you can now solve for the percentage of the total annual expenditures using the following equation:

**Total Annual Expenditures Percentage =
100% – _____ (Total Annual Allocations Percentage)
which results in _____
(Total Annual Expenditures Percentage)**

Step 5: You can now update your gross annual salary table with the number you've determined (the percentage of total annual expenditures).

	Annual Dollar Amount	Percentage of Gross Annual Salary
Total Annual Expenditures	$_____ (Enter Your Total Annual Expenditures)	_____% (Enter Your Percentage of Total Annual Expenditures)
Total Annual Allocations	$_____	_____% (Enter Your Total Allocations Percentage)
Gross Annual Salary	$_____	**100%**

Gross Annual Salary Table

Step 6: Now that you have both the annual dollar amount and the percentage of gross annual salary for the total annual expenditures, you can determine the gross annual salary:

Gross Annual Salary = Total Annual Expenditures dollar amount divided by decimal equivalent of Total Annual Expenditures percentage of gross annual salary

The resulting equation is:
Gross Annual Salary = $_____ divided by 0.___

Completing the above calculation will now allow you to update the Gross Annual Salary Table with the total for your tween's gross annual salary:

	Annual Dollar Amount	Percentage of Gross Annual Salary
Total Annual Expenditures	$_____ (Enter Your Total Annual Expenditures)	_____% (Enter Your Percentage of Total Annual Expenditures)
Total Annual Allocations	$_____	_____% (Enter Your Total Allocations Percentage)
Gross Annual Salary	**$_____ (Enter Your Gross Annual Salary**	**100%**

Gross Annual Salary Table

Step 7: In order to complete the table below, use the following equation:

Total Annual Allocations =
Gross Annual Salary – Total Annual Expenditures

With the number determined for the annual dollar amount of your total annual allocations, you can now complete the Gross Annual Salary Table:

	Annual Dollar Amount	Percentage of Gross Annual Salary
Total Annual Expenditures	$_____ (Enter Your Total Annual Expenditures)	_____% (Enter Your Percentage of Total Annual Expenditures)
Total Annual Allocations	$_____ (Enter Your Total Annual Allocations)	_____% (Enter Your Total Allocations Percentage)
Gross Annual Salary	**$_____ (Enter Your Gross Annual Salary**	**100%**

Gross Annual Salary Table

Step 8: Now that you have determined the gross annual salary, the final step in calculating your tween's paycheck is to divide the gross annual salary by the number of times you plan to pay your tween each year. The pay interval between those paychecks will be based on what you believe will be most convenient for you and your family. The following list represents the most likely pay intervals and total payments during the year:

Pay monthly = 12
Pay twice monthly (e.g., fifteenth and last day) = 24
Pay every two weeks = 26
Pay weekly = 52

With the pay interval you have chosen, you can now determine the gross salary paycheck:

Gross Salary Paycheck = _____
(Your Gross Annual Salary) divided by _____
(Pay Interval Number)

Step 9: Now that you know the specific dollar amounts for your tween's paycheck, you can determine the dollar amounts for each allocation, using the percentage you previously assigned to each.

Gross Pay (Enter your Gross Salary Paycheck amount)	$
Allocation for Injury Prevention (using your % to arrive at the dollar amount)	- $
Allocation for Long-Term Savings (using your % to arrive at the dollar amount)	-$
Allocation for 401(k)* (using your % to arrive at the dollar amount)	- $
Allocation for Charity (using your % to arrive at the dollar amount)	- $
Net Pay	$

*If you are matching your tween's 401(k) accounts, you will need to match the dollar amount for each paycheck from your own funds, so that the total deposit into this account will be double.

Having reached this point, you can breathe a big sigh of relief. Now that you know the amounts of your tween's paychecks, the allocation accounts and the amounts that you will put into each of them, and the net pay that your tween will receive, the rest of the journey should be enjoyable. What remains for you to do is to complete the setup and rollout of the program, and this is where the fun begins.

COMPANY NAME

One of the most enjoyable tasks in setting up this program is to determine the name of the company you want to use. This name has no bearing on the details of the program other than how you will refer to it when you talk with your tween, your other kids, and potentially your future grandkids. The reason I mention grandkids is that your kids may choose to use the same name when they teach their kids about money in the future.

For some of us, it is not easy to be creative when it comes to names. In fact, when my kids were toddlers, they wanted to name their black-and-white guinea pig "Blacky-Whitey." Now, how creative was that? It was through a simple family brainstorming exercise, during which we explored things that were both black and white, that we chose the name "Oreo."

You certainly can use the name "Money Athletics Program," which would be a rather noble choice, but going through the exercise of creating a unique company name is an opportunity to personalize the program for your family. I highly encourage you to make this task the first activity you do together with your tween at the time you roll out the program or shortly thereafter.

The best way to come up with the perfect company name is to follow a similar simple brainstorming exercise, just as we did to name our guinea pig. Think about adjectives and attributes that describe your family. What do you all enjoy doing? Do you enjoy sports together? How about music, a favorite book, favorite games, or a favorite place? How about attributes that relate to your family's heritage or the culture from which your family comes? The exercise could simply consist of creating a large list of words that are meaningful to your family and adding the word "Incorporated" at the end. The key to enjoying this first task is to limit the rules and have fun with it. Just like the basic rules of brainstorming, remember that no idea is a bad one, and every idea can build upon other ideas.

OFFER LETTER

Oftentimes when someone starts a new job, that person is presented with an offer letter that outlines the parameters of that job, the starting salary, and benefits. Not every company or job provides an offer letter, but I think it is a useful tool for introducing this program to your tween. I suggest that you present an offer letter to your son or daughter during the program rollout meeting.

The offer letter is the means whereby you present the details of the plan to your tween. It sets forth the items we just covered regarding the amount of pay and the allocations and expenses your tween will be responsible for managing. The offer letter is intended to resemble the type of letter your son or daughter might receive from a company in the future.

It's important to keep the offer letter short and simple while presenting an overview of the program that you are about to implement. It should summarize the items you will explain in more detail during the meeting.

Generally, receiving an offer letter is an exhilarating event, so presenting it in an exciting manner will make it even more meaningful and memorable for your tween. The following offer letter represents what I put together and presented to my kids when we rolled out the program.

Money Athletics Program
December 17, 2006

Scott Kaley
Address
City, State, Zip

RE: Offer

I/We are pleased to offer you the position of executive of the Money Athletics Program. Your position will start on January 1. Your compensation will consist of the following:

Monthly Salary of $175.

Allocations:

Each month the following allocations will be deducted from your paycheck on your behalf and deposited to the following accounts:

Gross Monthly Pay	$175.00
Allocation for Injury Prevention (10%)	- $17.50
Allocation for Long-Term Savings (10%)	- $17.50
Allocation for 401(k)* (10%)	- $17.50
Allocation for Charity (10%)	- $17.50
Net Pay (60%)	**$105.00**

*We will match this amount and add it to your account each pay period.

Expenses:

The net pay from the above table represents the amount you will have to cover expense items in the categories below. You will be responsible for deciding the amount to spend for each.

Item
Allowance and Entertainment
Clothing and Shoes
Birthday Party Gifts to Friends
Hot Lunches at School
School Supplies

We are delighted to offer you this position and allow us to share your journey toward financial fitness!

Love,
Your Parent(s)

The following is a blank offer letter for your reference. You can find a blank offer letter template on the MoneyAthletics.com website that you are welcome to download and use as your starting point.

Your desired company name

Month Day, Year
Your Tween's Name
Address
City, State, Zip

RE: Offer

I/We are pleased to offer you the position of executive of the (your desired company name). Your position will start on (enter month and day). Your compensation will consist of the following:

Monthly Salary of $

Allocations:
Each pay period the following allocations will be deducted from your paycheck on your behalf and deposited to the following accounts:

Gross Pay	$
Allocation for Injury Prevention Fund (__%)	- $
Allocation for Long-Term Savings (__%)	- $
Allocation for 401(k)* (__%)	- $
Allocation for Charity (__%)	- $
Net Pay (__%)	$

*We will match this amount and add it to your account each pay period.

Expenses:

The net pay from the above table represents the amount you will have to cover expense items in the following categories. You will be responsible for deciding the amount to spend for each:

Item
Allowance and Entertainment
Clothing and Shoes
Birthday Party Gifts to Friends
Hot Lunches at School
School Supplies

We are delighted to offer you this position and that you are willing to allow us to share your journey toward financial fitness!

Love,
Your Parent(s)

Make the Offer and Make It a Big Deal!

Do you remember when you received your driver's license? What about the first movie you saw without your parents? The first record album or CD you bought? Do you remember how exciting each of those moments was? Well, what you are about to do with your tween will become a memorable moment for both of you as your son or daughter begins the journey toward becoming financially fit. For that reason, I encourage you to make the presentation of the offer letter a big deal. Presenting it in some grand way helps to elevate the enthusiasm around the conversation you will have with your tween.

If the rollout timeframe happens to coincide with a birthday or a holiday such as Christmas, you can use those times to help make it a big deal by providing it as a present. For all three of my kids, we happened to roll it out in December, so it coincided with the Christmas season. However, there is no need to tie it to a particular event or holiday. The significance of the rollout is that you are acknowledging what is happening in their lives—that they are progressing on their journey to becoming young adults. Growing their financial skills will pave the way for a smoother road.

In order to have a successful and meaningful rollout, set aside time for the conversation about the program. I suggest at least one hour. Some families I've worked with went out to eat at a restaurant and had the conversation over a meal. The most important consideration is to hold the rollout meeting in a place that will allow you to have an important and exciting conversation with your tween with the least amount of interruption.

We had the conversation with our two oldest kids at the same time since we rolled out the program to them together. I kicked off the conversation by highlighting a few things that I knew my kids were frustrated about at the time with regard to money. For example, they struggled with having to ask Mom or Dad for money when they wanted to buy things like clothes or when they wanted to buy something online. I began by asking, "Would you like to have more freedom to manage your money so that you don't have to ask us for money?" I could see my kids' eyes light up. I acknowledged that I knew they did not like having to ask for money and proceeded to discuss that as one grows older and moves toward becoming a young adult, it is important to have good money skills. "Would you both like to have good money skills and be able to start making decisions that are more grown-up?" I asked.

"Yes!" they enthusiastically replied.

I then provided each of them with their offer letter, which highlighted the key aspects of the program. We discussed each allocation item as well as the expenses they would be responsible for managing. Interestingly, the number that stood out to them was that they would have $105 to spend each month. The rest of the program did not necessarily sink in at that time. I was not surprised; because of their age, I expected such a response—I was certain that almost every tween would react the same way. To my amusement and delight, I could see the excitement in their eyes as unspoken questions floated by such as "How much candy can I buy?" and "How many toys can I get?"

I explained that they would have the freedom to make their own financial decisions, but with that freedom would come a great deal of responsibility. That responsibility would include paying for the items that were on the expense list. I also explained that they would likely have to develop a budget for some of those items, such as clothing and school supplies.

After the explanation of the program, which the offer letter helped me facilitate, the questions started pouring out. "How do we get the money?" "When do we get the money?" They even posed some questions around the allocations for savings and the 401(k). There was definitely a lot of excitement and enthusiasm to get started.

I expect that your tween will react in much the same way. Be ready for their exuberant reaction and those initial questions as they attempt to wrap their minds around this very big "adult" step that is about to happen in their tween lives. As part of the rollout meeting, once your tweens have begun to settle into the idea of what lies ahead for them, you can take the opportunity to brainstorm a family company name while everyone is together. If that seems like too much to tackle because of the excitement level, then enjoy the celebration and schedule another time to come back together to identify a name prior to their first Money Athletics adventure trip.

The next phase of the rollout with your tween is best described through what took place in our family as we went on their initial Money Athletics adventure trips, established their accounts, and conducted their first action steps.

SETTING UP ACCOUNTS

The first Money Athletics adventure trip with my kids was to set up their bank accounts—a very different experience from other visits to the bank with them. In the past, they had taken trips with us to the bank but never really thought much about what it meant to be there, except that they always received a lollipop from the bank teller while they were there. In fact, they thought of the bank as the lollipop place and were excited when we occasionally brought them along. This time, they would still be able to receive a lollipop from the teller, but they would first be required to participate in the reason for our visit.

We met with a new account representative at our bank and asked to set up accounts on behalf of each child. Each account required a minimal initial deposit. The following accounts, all of which would have online access capabilities, represent the initial accounts we established that day.

1. **Checking account, with attached Visa debit/ATM card.** This would be the account they would use for expense spending.
2. **Savings account for injury prevention.** This would become their emergency savings account.
3. **Savings account for long-term savings.** This would become their savings for long-term spending—in our kids' case, spending money for college.
4. **Charity account.** This would become their savings account where they could disperse funds to their desired charitable causes.

The bank representative printed out a number of forms that I and both my son and daughter had to sign. My kids were certainly feeling more grown-up as they signed each form. As their parent, I was required to be a co-owner of each account and needed to sign each of the forms along with them. It took about thirty minutes to set up everything. We were told that it would take about a week to get the checks for the checking account and the Visa debit card and that those would come in the mail. As we left the bank, both kids received a lollipop. Dad got one too.

ONLINE ACCESS, DIRECT DEPOSITS, AND TRANSFERS

It only took a day for us to be able to access their accounts through the Internet. When I logged into my account, I could see the new accounts on my account summary screen. I changed the generic names of the new accounts so they would have names that helped me distinguish one from the other when I accessed them online. My summary screen of accounts looked like the following:

Deposit Accounts (as of 12/18/2006)			
Account Name	**Account #**	**Current Balance**	**Available Balance**
Craig & Karen's Checking	XXXXXX7624		

Craig & Karen's Injury Prevention Savings	XXXXXX3691		
Craig & Karen's Long-Term Savings	XXXXXX5683		
Craig & Karen's Charity Savings	XXXXXX1274		
Scott's Checking	XXXXXX5915		
Scott's Injury Prevention Savings	XXXXXX7207		
Scott's Long-Term Savings	XXXXXX5829		
Scott's Charity Savings	XXXXXX0302		
Nicole's Checking	XXXXXX6445		
Nicole's Injury Prevention Savings	XXXXXX8997		
Nicole's Long-Term Savings	XXXXXX8654		
Nicole's Charity Savings	XXXXXX8872		

The account that didn't show up here was the 401(k) savings account. As previously mentioned, the 401(k) accounts we set up for our son and daughter were actually 529 college savings plans. Those accounts were managed at a different financial institution from our bank.

Since I had access to everything online, I was able to set up all of the electronic transfers for each of my tweens. I matched everything as had been outlined in their offer letters. I set up recurring transfers to occur on the first of every month from my checking account into their various accounts.

Here is the list of those automatic transfers:

1. Transfer $17.50 from my checking to Scott's injury prevention savings.
2. Transfer $17.50 from my checking to Scott's long-term savings.
3. Transfer $17.50 from my checking to Scott's charity savings.
4. Transfer/Bill Pay $35.00 from my checking to Scott's 401(k) (college 529 plan).
5. Transfer $105.00 from my checking to Scott's checking account.
6. Transfer $17.50 from my checking to Nicole's injury prevention savings.
7. Transfer $17.50 from my checking to Nicole's long-term savings.
8. Transfer $17.50 from my checking to Nicole's charity savings.
9. Transfer/Bill Pay $35.00 from my checking to Nicole's 401(k) (college 529 plan).

10. Transfer $105.00 from my checking to Nicole's checking account.

Once I finished the setup, I knew the hard work was behind us. Everything would now transfer automatically each month, and my son, daughter, and I wouldn't have to think about it. However, one thing I discovered early on was that my son and daughter always knew exactly when the transfers were scheduled to occur. In fact, they continually got excited when their payday rolled around.

THE NEXT MONEY ATHLETICS ADVENTURE TRIPS

Approximately a week went by, and we received the checks and the debit cards for both my son and daughter. I could hardly wait for our next three Money Athletics adventure trips. We happened to combine these three trips into one longer trip since I wanted to capitalize on their excitement. There is nothing wrong, however, with spacing out the trips should that be more convenient and optimal for your children's learning experience—many parents choose to do it that way.

The adventure trip with my children included a return trip to the bank to learn how to do a deposit and a withdrawal and to learn how to use the ATM for withdrawing cash or making a deposit. We also made a stop at a store so they could learn how to make a purchase with their debit card. Each stop on our adventure trip was fun and provided a great learning experience for my kids. It was their chance to participate in grown-up activities.

Trip to the Bank

The adventure trip I took with my son and daughter back to the bank coincided with the holiday season. Since it was close to Christmas, I wrote each of my kids a check for $25 so they could deposit it into their checking account.

With their gift checks in hand, we entered the bank. I took them to the desk where we had to fill out a deposit slip. The deposit slip required that they fill out the date, the amount of the deposit, and their checking account number. I also explained how they needed to sign the back of the check.

My son Scott spent a lot of time filling out each part and asked me as he completed each step whether he'd done it correctly. Being a rule follower, Scott has always gotten nervous about doing things wrong, whether it was in school, in sports, or in almost any situation. When Scott had finished filling out his deposit slip and had signed his check, I turned to help my daughter, who had been standing right next to me. She wasn't there because she'd already completed everything and was talking with a bank teller about depositing her check. That's exactly how my daughter has always done things. She listens to how things need to be done and then dives in. She rarely asks if things have been done correctly. She assumes she's done them right the first time and moves on without hesitation.

As Scott went up to the bank teller, Nicole was just finishing her deposit and had already received her deposit receipt. She then went to stand next to Scott so she could offer him help in case he had any questions. She was now the expert. Scott successfully made his deposit and received his deposit receipt as well. We proceeded to walk out of the bank, but not before each of us grabbed a lollipop.

Trip to the ATM

The next stop was the ATM machine. When we left the bank, we drove to a location that had a walk-up ATM. Since this was their first time using an ATM machine, I wanted to use a walk-up ATM so that I could show them the screens and how to use them. It would have been difficult to use a drive-up ATM and show them how the process worked.

When we received the Visa debit/ATM card in the mail after we opened their accounts, we also had to wait for the personal ID number to arrive. That information came in a separate mailing but within a day or so of receiving the card. Both children memorized that number before we visited the ATM.

The goal of this visit to the ATM was to withdraw $20. My daughter went first and inserted her card into the ATM machine. The next screen asked her to enter her PIN. She successfully did that, and the following screen displayed the options from which she could choose. They included making a withdrawal, making a deposit, and obtaining an account balance.

I explained each option to them and told them that since we wanted to get $20 in cash, we would select the withdrawal option. Nicole selected that option, and the next screen asked whether to withdraw from checking or savings. Since their checking account was their spending account, I told them to select checking. After she chose the checking option, the next question she needed to answer was how much she wanted to withdraw. I explained that ATM machines only stock $20 bills, so the amount they withdrew would need to be $20, $40, $60, or larger increments of $20. She selected $20, and then the magic happened as a $20 bill was dispensed from the machine.

The last couple of questions she needed to answer were whether she wanted to do another transaction and whether she wanted a transaction receipt. I said that they should always get a receipt when they withdrew cash so they would be able to remember to enter the withdrawal into their checking account register in order to keep an accurate account balance.

Next, it was my son's turn. Having watched his sister, the process was no longer a mystery for Scott. In fact, he simply followed all the prompts and had his $20 in no time. The ATM leg of our adventure trip was a huge success!

Purchase at a Store with the Debit Card

We left the ATM machine and proceeded to our local grocery store. The goal was to buy something small, such as some candy, using their debit card. With their confidence running high from the first two stops, I expected this one to be uneventful. In fact, I expected it to be a straightforward process for the two of them. However, I received a glaring look from the customer waiting in line immediately behind us.

Both Scott and Nicole grabbed a pack of gum from the display next to the checkout stand. Scott proceeded to the cashier. The cashier rang up the pack of gum, and Scott provided his debit card for payment. The cashier swiped the card because we were using it like a credit card. Scott then needed to sign his name on the signature pad. Within a few minutes, he was done with his purchase and had his receipt and pack of gum in hand. Next, Nicole did the same transaction. I am not sure what it was about my daughter, but although this was her first transaction with a debit card, I was amazed at her confidence and the naturalness of her actions as she completed the purchase transaction.

I mentioned that I received a glaring look from a customer in line behind us. To add to the glare was a comment she made to me: "You are setting your kids up for failure by giving them credit cards at such a young age!" I gave her a quick smile and said nothing as we proceeded to the exit. Little did that woman know that I was doing the exact opposite for my kids! If only she could see my kids today and the financial confidence they both possess. If she only knew she was seeing them on the very first day of their financial journey to becoming financially fit young adults.

It's Your Turn!

How you will approach setting up your tweens' accounts and the steps you will take to help them gain understanding, experience, and confidence as they embark on this journey toward financial independence may look different from what we did in my family or they may occur in a different order. What's essential is that your tweens be involved with opening their accounts and, once those accounts are established and they receive their debit card and PIN, that they have the opportunity to learn how to deposit and withdraw from the bank and ATM as well as how to make purchases in a store. Keep in mind that something we do as adults almost every day, and which may seem mundane and even rote to us, is going to open your child to a whole new world. Keep it light, and above all else, make it fun and memorable!

CHAPTER CHECKLIST

✓ Determine the final salary amount.

✓ Develop an offer letter.

✓ Make the offer and make it a big deal.

✓ Identify your company name.

✓ Take your kids to the bank to set up their accounts.

✓ Set up the automated deposits and transfers into your tweens' accounts.

✓ Take your tweens on their first several field trips:
- To the bank to make an initial deposit
- To an ATM machine to make a deposit and a withdrawal
- To a store to make a purchase with their debit card

6

YOU IN THE ROLE OF COACH

Congratulations, you have now completed the setup and rollout of the Money Athletics Program for your tween. Although the details of your program have been ironed out, your tween's journey toward financial fitness, and your role to help him or her achieve it, is just beginning. In order for your tween to learn the concepts of the Money Athletics Program, a knowledgeable teacher is required. And in order for your son or daughter to fully integrate this program into day-to-day life, each child will benefit most by having a steadfast coach. My intention in this chapter is to give you some perspective on how you can be a great financial teacher and coach so that your son or daughter will be successful.

What might surprise you about being a great financial coach is that the attributes that make a great coach have more to do with you being an approachable teacher and mentor than needing to have in-depth financial knowledge. The money skills your tween will be learning are the same skills you practice every day—such as saving, spending, balancing accounts, and planning for the future. For that reason, you are already the expert your son or daughter needs you to be for this journey.

Initially, I was worried about being a great coach for my kids, but as we progressed through the program, I discovered I could answer and help with virtually everything they had questions about, and when I was uncertain, I could easily find answers by doing a search on the Internet. My financial confidence grew as I helped my kids learn about money.

Leading up to the writing of this chapter, I saw a documentary on the great football coach Vince Lombardi. There are certainly a lot of powerful quotes that live on from him regarding great leadership, but what I learned most from the documentary was how his players felt about him and what they said about how he influenced them over the course of their lives—not just on the football field. Along with many valuable lessons, Coach Lombardi taught them how to "give their all" in anything they did as well as to understand the importance of character. His biggest focus, however, was on the significance of mastering the basics. That really struck a chord with me, as becoming great at anything—whether in a particular sport, musical instrument, reading, writing, math, or any other subject—requires that a person have a solid grasp of the basics.

I realized that mastery is what the Money Athletics Program is really all about—starting early and mastering the basics of money. To help your tween master the basics, you do not need to be a Coach Lombardi or any other famous coach. You simply need to be the mom or dad to your tween that you are already and help coach your son or daughter through the Money Athletics process you've set up, which in turn will help your tween master the basics. Let's look at some key components that will help your child best respond to you as a coach.

1. Coaches understand and build confidence.

As the parent of your tween, you understand the personality traits of your son or daughter better than anyone else. The most important trait needed for your tween to become financially fit is confidence. Early on in the program, your tweens may not have a lot of confidence about money because it is something new to them. However, every day that goes by under their own money management will build their confidence, not only for their immediate money needs, but also for their future.

As an example, I recently spoke to Stacy, a mother who implemented this program when her son, Zjelko, who was thirteen years old. At the time, he had minimal understanding of how to manage his own money and how to make key decisions about saving, planning, and budgeting. He is now sixteen years old and has a level of confidence to manage money that many adults would be envious of. Stacy told me that Zjelko has a strong desire to go to medical school. He realizes that the cost of doing so will be extremely high, and he will likely have to go into debt. However, he already has a plan to pay off his medical school loans, and he is only a sophomore in high school. With Zjelko's confidence growing in how to manage money, he will be able to think about possibilities for his future that go beyond finances.

2. Coaches should be tough but fair.

One of the hardest parts of being a parent is watching your kids struggle at something. This can happen when they are learning new topics in school, playing a sport, playing a musical instrument, or managing their own money. In fact, there will be many times when their frustration level will rise and you will see your son or daughter struggle.

Based on my experiences with my own kids, as well as what I've been told by other parents, the financial struggles in the tween years are oftentimes because your son or daughter does not have enough money to purchase something. As the parent and coach, these moments are key learning opportunities and occasions when you'll most likely be called upon to be tough but fair.

For instance, instead of caving in and buying something for them, this is the perfect opportunity to engage in a conversation about how your tweens can solve the issue. Be realistic and honest about what your tweens can achieve— even when doing so is hard. It's important to not criticize them, but rather to look at and address the situation. It may not feel like it at the time, but your son or daughter will eventually look up to you more for having helped as a guide through financial issues than if you simply bought something they requested.

In an earlier chapter, I mentioned that on one occasion my daughter did not have enough money for a birthday gift for her close friend. Through the tears she shed and the comments she made about how mean I was for not providing money to her, she was able to arrive at the decision to make a gift for her friend instead of buying one. The gift she created turned out to be one of the most cherished gifts her friend received.

Another example happened with my older son, Scott, when he was fourteen. He loved to play golf, and when the weather started to get warmer in the spring, he discovered that his golf club set was too small for him. He had grown a lot taller since the previous summer. Although he had done a good job of saving his money, he did not have enough to buy a new set. He asked if I would lend the money to him, and I said I would not. I could see the frustration on his face, but I asked him if we could work together to figure out a solution. The first thing we did was determine the specific set he wanted to get. Once we determined that, we discovered that he was only about fifty dollars short of what he needed. He was also about two weeks away from his next paycheck, which would provide him with adequate funds to purchase the golf clubs. We agreed that in two weeks we would go to the sporting goods store and purchase the set of clubs he wanted. Ironically, the next week in the Sunday paper, there was a flyer from the sporting goods store advertising that the golf club set he wanted was on sale for seventy-five dollars off. I shared the flyer with Scott and asked him, "What do you think about going to the store today?" Of course, his eyes lit up. We went to the store that day, and he was able to get his new set of clubs.

I am not suggesting that waiting to make a purchase always results in the item going on sale. I am suggesting that the process of discussing the situation, looking at what he could afford and how much more money he needed, set the stage for him to make a quick decision when the sale happened. He was in control the whole time. Even if the clubs had never gone on sale, he would have bought them after he received his paycheck. I know he would have felt proud of his ability to plan and make the purchase either way. And I felt like a good coach as we drove home with the golf clubs. Together, on that same day, we even went to the driving range so he could try them out. It was fun and satisfying for me to see the pride on his face, knowing that he'd planned for and made the purchase himself.

3. Coaches teach life skills, not just money skills.

I remember when Scott was born and I became a parent for the first time. Boy, was I scared! I felt like I didn't know what I was doing in those first days of his life. I didn't know how to change a diaper, how to give him a bath, how to feed him, and so much more. What I did know was that I could and would persevere through my mistakes and, in a very short timeframe, become good at those very things that initially scared me. I also realized that so much of parenting was about going through life's journey with my kids, not as an expert, but as an amateur coach and mentor. Sometimes I was only one day smarter about a topic than my kids. For example, when I became my son's soccer coach when he was five years old, many times on the night before a game or practice, I read and researched how to run a particular practice drill, play, or strategy.

I read many books on parenting to become better in as many areas as I could—not only about how to raise a son or daughter, but most of all about how to raise a great young adult. Long before I became inspired about the Money Athletics Program, I focused on teaching life skills to my kids and being the best parent I could be. It turned out that those same life skills I impressed upon my kids were the foundation for great money skills. Although the Money Athletics Program focuses on teaching kids about money skills—such as planning, persevering, focusing, and practicing—remember that those same skills carry over to many other facets of life.

4. Coaches should never be demeaning.

The best coaches and teachers many of us have experienced in life can be described as having similar attributes. Most likely, we would say they were tough and inspiring, they imparted knowledge in a clear, straightforward manner, and somehow they knew how to get the best out of us. Most of us would never say that a great coach was demeaning to us. If the coach was, the desired result would have been lost.

A real-life illustration comes to mind related to my son Scott. Scott was the placekicker for his high school football team, kicking the ball to score extra points and field goals for the team. He demonstrated great talent as a freshman, and by the end of the season, he was brought up to the varsity team to kick during the playoffs. The following season, during his sophomore year, he kicked throughout the entire season and did very well for a tenth grader on the team. However, during one of the last games of that season, he had a bad game in which he missed a field goal and two extra points. After he missed the last one and walked off the field, I watched the coach scream at him for almost a whole minute and drop multiple f-bombs, literally cutting Scott to shreds. My son never fully recovered from that game and decided not to play football again after that season. How sad! Did the coach even know what he had done, and did he even care? I wish I knew those answers.

What was reinforced in me after that experience was how the act of cutting down and demeaning somebody can have a profound effect on the person. I was determined to make sure I never did that to my kids. Instead, I focused my attention on inspiring them to learn about managing their money and on growing their confidence.

Your tweens are learning the life skill to manage their own finances, yet they can be fragile during this learning process. It's important for you to be encouraging, but do not push too hard or too fast as they progress through their money learning journey. Remember, the foundation of this program is to learn money basics *over time*. Unfortunately, as parents, and in our enthusiasm to impart wisdom and see our children succeed, we can sometimes push too hard and cause our kids to lose interest in the very activity they once loved. For instance, consider the aspiring baseball player who stops playing because he can't seem to hit a curve ball or the dancer who quits because she is frustrated when she can't seem to get the timing right for a particular move.

The same can happen when we are teaching our children about money. As your tweens' coach, it is important to lift them up instead of knock them down. For instance, it is not necessary, or even advisable, to tell your tween that he or she was stupid for writing a check that caused an overdraft in the account. When you think about it, most of us have made those mistakes at some time in our lives. The better approach is to acknowledge the event, work together to understand why it happened, and then strategize to make improvements for the future. In all cases, when a teaching opportunity prevails, ask your son or daughter, "How can we work together on this issue?"

5. Coaches makes mistake too.

One of the most humbling parts of this program is that there will be times when, as the coach, you will make a mistake. What I learned is that being open about making those mistakes can be just as powerful a learning experience as when the lesson is rooted in something your tween does or doesn't do.

The best way to illustrate this is through an example. The year after I rolled out the Money Athletics Program to my two oldest kids, we went on a family vacation to the Pacific Northwest. We toured Yellowstone, then traveled to Seattle, down to Portland, and back to Denver. It took about twelve days, during which time we covered over three thousand miles. To this day, we all remember that trip as one of our best family vacations. Everyone also remembers a very specific incident that occurred while we were driving near Portland. I got pulled over for speeding. I must admit that I had received speeding tickets before, but this was the first time I had received one with the whole family in the vehicle. The kids paid close attention to the whole process, and after the police officer handed me the ticket and I read the details, I revealed to them the amount of the fine, $175 dollars.

After we drove away and I relaxed a little, the kids started to ask a lot of questions about the process of getting pulled over for speeding, including how fast I was going. However, my son then hit me with this: "Dad, how are you going to pay for that ticket? Have you been funding your injury prevention account?" Believe it or not, my son had busted me! The kids laughed at me hysterically, and all I could do was take it, which I did. Since this was soon after the inception of our program, I did not yet have everything in place that I could have had, and maybe should have had. I then confessed and explained to them that because I did not have that account set up and funded, the ticket would impact our finances. I told them that we would have to forego some dinners out at a restaurant or cut back in other areas. I recall thinking to myself how impressed I was with my kids that they'd just busted me with great insight and an understanding of what we'd put in place for them. I knew going forward that they would keep me on my toes as much as I would be trying to keep them on theirs.

You will likely make mistakes as part of this program and possibly find yourself playing catch-up in your personal family finances, so I encourage you to gracefully own up to any mistakes you make as well as acknowledge your own learning curve. Take those opportunities and turn them into learning experiences for your children. Some of those instances may actually become funny moments to laugh about together and places to find lightness in the midst of a subject that can at times get heavy.

CHAPTER CHECKLIST

✓ Understand that your tween needs a coach and wants a great one who is empathetic.

✓ Keep in mind that it is all about building money confidence.

✓ Consider that there will be times when you need to be tough but fair.

✓ Remember that what you are imparting is as much about life skills as it is money skills.

✓ Make it a habit to never be demeaning.

✓ Know that you will make mistakes too.

STRENGTH TRAINING

In the last chapter, we discussed how you, in the role of a money coach, contribute to your son's or daughter's learning. Recalling the 70:20:10 rule, the bulk of your child's learning will come from practice. This chapter is all about the ways you might capitalize on learning opportunities when they arise and how to create other opportunities to strengthen your tween's money skills.

It's important that you make the most of the opportunities that present themselves naturally, but your tween will also benefit from opportunities that you create with Money Athletics adventure trips. Learning opportunities happen as part of everyday life, while adventure trips are activities that you create to set the stage for your tween to learn about a specific topic.

Below are some highlights of key areas to draw upon for strength training.

CAPITALIZE ON NATURAL LEARNING OPPORTUNITIES

It was not long after we rolled out the Money Athletics Program to our two oldest kids that we were all sitting in front of the TV and a major credit card-issuing company commercial came on. The slogan of this particular card company was "The card that pays you back!" The commercial stated that the more you use your credit card, the more you'll make. In the past, I normally tuned out these commercials; however, my son and daughter both asked how a credit card-issuing company pays a person for using a card. That question took me by surprise, since I was not expecting such an insightful inquiry so soon after my kids started into the program.

I quickly realized that this was an amazing opportunity to teach them about credit cards. It also gave me the chance to explain how credit card-issuing companies try to entice people to use their cards. I explained to the two of them the basics of how credit cards work and how credit card-issuing companies make their money. I approached the matter with some key points.

There are three primary ways that credit card-issuing companies make money:

1. The first is that they charge the store, or seller, a percentage fee for using the credit card. In most cases, this is about 2 percent of the transaction amount, so for every ten dollars you spend, roughly twenty cents is paid to the

credit card-issuing company and other supporting services. I asked my kids how much the credit card-issuing company makes if you buy a pair of jeans for thirty dollars. What about when someone uses a credit card to buy fifty dollars' worth of groceries? After multiple scenarios like this, my kids understood that a small amount of every credit card transaction is paid by the seller to the credit card-issuing company.

2. The second way credit card-issuing companies make money is by charging interest on the unpaid balance of your credit card bill, usually a very high interest rate that can be 20 percent or more. Again, using an example to illustrate this, I explained the following: "Let's say you spend $100 in a month using a credit card. If you do not pay off the full amount at the end of every month, the credit card-issuing company requires you to pay interest on that amount. That interest is added to your bill each month"

I highlighted that credit cards are a very expensive way to pay for things if you do not pay the full bill every month. I also highlighted that debit cards are different. With a debit card, the money has to be in your account first, whereas a credit card-issuing company allows you to spend money you don't have. That is where it becomes dangerous.

3. The third way credit card-issuing companies make money is by charging fees for actions such as going over your credit (spending) limit and paying late. These fees can be very expensive. I then provided the following example. "Let's say that your credit card spending limit is $200 and you spend $210, or ten dollars over your limit. The card company can charge you a fee of $25 for going over your limit. It can

then add another $25 if you don't make your payment on time. So imagine having to pay $50 in one month for those two mistakes!"

After explaining these three key points about how credit card-issuing companies make money, I saw that both my son and daughter had perplexed looks on their faces.

My kids said that it seemed that the credit card-issuing companies charged a lot of money to use their credit cards.

"Yes, they do," I responded. "However, if you always pay off the amount you use, and you always pay on time, then you can receive benefits such as the 'cash back' that the commercial was talking about."

"How much cash back could you get?" asked one.

"About 1 percent to 1.5 percent is usually all that they pay back."

The unimpressed look on their faces was a treasure to behold as they began to grasp how credit cards work and how dangerous they can be, especially for an eleven- and twelve-year-old.

◎ ◎ ◎

There are many natural learning opportunities, such as the one I've described, that will present themselves through TV, newspapers, magazines, and websites. These are great times to engage in conversations about the various companies that advertise, how those companies make money, and how they can impact us. In fact, it is fair to say that almost every advertisement, commercial, or solicitation has an angle to get you to spend money. Some examples that will spark good conversations include the following:

- **Store sales**—Are you really saving money? Highlight that stores are always having sales.

- **Small monthly payments for items**—This is common for infomercials and even car commercials. Based upon the number of payments, is the product really being offered at a good price?

- **Banks and credit card-issuing companies**—Many will operate in a way similar to the example I gave earlier, but to further entice you to use their services, they may offer lower fees, including "free checking," smaller interest rates on credit cards, and lower interest rates on loans that you may acquire from the bank.

- **Insurance companies**—Many kids do not understand the concept of insurance; however, these companies advertise a lot. It would be good to converse with your son or daughter about how paying an insurance company a fee every month can help protect you in the event something goes wrong. I used an example of how insurance protects us by describing what would happen if their bicycles were stolen. I told them that although we hope that scenario never happens, if it did, the insurance company would help to pay for replacements. I then explained that car insurance companies are very similar. Although the advertisements don't necessarily state how much the insurance will cost, those ads can lead to another great conversation about how insurance companies make money. The details of why insurance is important and the role it plays in one's finances is something that will be discussed in the next book in the Moneyletics Series. *Money All-Stars* focuses on growing money skills for teenagers by building upon the skills you develop in your tweens with this program.

- **Airline companies**—Airlines often advertise how much it will cost to go from one city to another. Engaging in a discussion about the overall cost to go away somewhere will test your kids. Besides the flight, what about the costs of a hotel and rental car when you get there? What about the costs of food and any entertainment expenses? How much would it cost to drive, taking into account the miles and the cost of gasoline?

- **Charities**—There are many charities that advertise. They may even call your home phone or ring your doorbell. If you have decided to make charity a part of your tween's Money Athletics Program, having a conversation about the charities that matter to him or her is time well spent. In your conversation, consider things like the manner in which those charities make money. Additionally, how much of the raised money actually goes to the cause versus the amounts that go to advertising and other administrative expenses?

Initially, I wasn't tuned in to the opportunities for these types of discussions, but as my kids started to advance in their money skills, it became obvious that such opportunities were abundant. I just needed to open my eyes and ears and pay attention to what was all around us. By staying tuned in, you will see many relevant occasions for great learning discussions with your tween.

Learning Opportunities Can Pop Up Anytime

At times, you may be ready for natural learning opportunities to present themselves, such as when you are watching TV, shopping online, reading a magazine, or even when you are all riding in the car and see a billboard sign. Sometimes, however, the opportunities can sneak up on you. By simply having an open mind and making time for the circumstances, these unexpected opportunities can turn into terrific learning events.

For instance, when my son Scott was fourteen, our dishwasher started to leak every time we ran it. He and I got a flashlight and tried to investigate where the leak was coming from, but it was difficult to identify the spot. Both Scott and I discussed what we should do. If we called a repair company, it would charge close to $150 dollars just to have someone walk through the door. The parts and repair would likely add more to the cost, possibly another $100 or more, so we concluded that to fix the dishwasher would entail a minimum of $250 in repair costs. Even though I did have some funds in my injury prevention account, thanks to the verbal abuse I had received from my kids on our vacation, it was still more than I wanted to spend. Reluctantly, though, I called and scheduled a repair service visit.

The repairperson was able to come on a Saturday morning when both Scott and I were home. We explained to the repairperson the issue and watched how he troubleshot the problem. He stated that he would have to do some research and come back to do the repair. He told us that he would call back on the following Monday, just two days later, and schedule a time. Well, Monday came and went, but the repairperson never called. By this time, the frustration had spread to all of us in the house because we still had to do the dishes by hand after every meal. Scott and I discussed whether we should consider simply buying a new dishwasher. We did some research online and determined that the cost of a comparable dishwasher would be about $525 dollars. That was more than twice what we thought the repair would cost. We were also thinking that the repair might be more complicated, so we concluded that it could cost more than the $250 we originally estimated. Then Scott had a great idea to do some searches on both Google and YouTube.

Although we did not find an exact repair solution for the problem with our dishwasher, we did gain enough confidence to embark on a new adventure. The two of us decided to take the dishwasher out and see if we could find the issue. My wife was a bit scared to see her husband and older son jump into an appliance repair project that she was sure would result in a new dishwasher.

We took the dishwasher out and turned it on its side to investigate the location of the leak in an effort to determine the cause. We discovered that there was an overflow drain located in the corner covered by a round plastic disc. We popped the disc off and found that a rubber washer and a plastic nut held the drain tube in place. The nut was so loose that we could turn it with a bare hand. We proceeded to tighten the nut. We then put everything back together and ran the dishwasher. High fives were in order because the dishwasher ran perfectly. Scott and I had fixed our dishwasher! And the icing on the cake—the total cost of the repairs equaled zero dollars. To celebrate our accomplishment and the money we saved, our whole family went out to eat that same night, which did not cost nearly what the repairs or a new dishwasher would have.

As a result of this experience, all of my kids and I try to determine if we can fix something first by researching the issue on the Internet through websites such as YouTube. If we can't fix the problem ourselves, only then do we feel the need to reach out to a repairperson.

What was especially interesting about this story was that I went into this situation thinking I would be working with my son to evaluate and make a sound financial decision regarding an unexpected expense. What transpired was completely different, but it was a learning experience nonetheless. In fact, he learned a lot about appliance repair companies and the challenges that can occur with them, and I learned that Google and YouTube are great resources for home repair projects. To this day, remembering the dishwasher repair experience, my son Scott offers to help me fix things around the house when they break.

ONGOING MONEY ATHLETICS ADVENTURE TRIPS

Involving your son or daughter in money decisions and spending activities is the spirit behind Money Athletics adventure trips. You already received a sneak peek about those in chapter 5 when we discussed the rollout of this program. Those adventures included going to the bank for the first time, then to the ATM machine, and finally to a store to make a purchase with a debit card.

As you continue with this program, the first key goal is simply to continue to engage your tween in the money activities that you experience, such as major purchases, vacation planning, and unexpected expenses.

The second key goal is for you to be a participant in the financial events that your tween encounters, mainly as a supporter and mentor, not as the decision-maker.

I do not have a specific set of trips to prescribe for you to experience with your tweens. Rather, I think it is more important to engage them in the scenarios that surface organically from the time you start them on the program and as you move forward.

Here are a few of the most memorable adventure trips that I encountered with my kids:

Gift-giving—I engaged my daughter in an adventure trip just a couple of months after we rolled out the program. I asked her to help me select a Valentine's Day gift for her mom. Unbeknownst to me at the time, I was about to unleash the shopping marvel that is my daughter. I shared with her the amount I was looking to spend and asked if she could help me find the right gift package that would be meaningful to her mother. Even at eleven years old, she proved to be a master of online shopping research. She was able to help me come up with a gift package of flowers, a gift card to a nail salon, and a dinner date out—all within the budget I had set. To this day, I still utilize her skills to help select gifts for Christmas, birthdays, and other events.

Spring break vacation—When my son was fourteen and my daughter was thirteen, we decided to go on a spring break trip to Arizona. We combined our trip with my son's out-of-state baseball tournament, and we planned to enjoy some family activities during our time away.

My wife and I engaged the help of our son and daughter to plan flights, identify hotel accommodations, and organize activities for us to do while we were there, all within a set budget. This allowed for family discussions about saving money on things like the rental car so we could stay at a nicer hotel. As a result of their research and our discussions, we decided to drive to Arizona instead of fly and rent a car. That decision provided us with more funds for additional activities we could all enjoy together.

Purchase of a new car for the family—While our kids were tweens, we found we were in need of a new family vehicle. Although my wife and I knew we would obtain an auto loan to buy the vehicle, we simplified things and included our kids in the decision-making process by explaining to them what payment we could afford. I felt they were still a bit young to get into the details about interest rates, loan terms, and leasing since those topics would not become important until they reached their later teenage years. Armed with how much we could afford, our son and daughter helped us go to the car dealer and determine what car would work best for our family. We also engaged in conversations around fuel economy since gas prices were approaching four dollars per gallon at the time. We considered how much more expensive a car would be if it had poor gas mileage.

As a parent, I didn't always know if a specific activity would be meaningful to my kids, but both my son and daughter remembered our car purchase, and when it came time to buy their own first vehicles, they were clear about the questions they needed to ask and factors they needed to consider. For example, my son bought a small pickup truck from a seller on Craigslist. He did all of the research and found the truck he wanted. On his own, he determined what he could afford. He told me that as he researched cars for himself, he remembered some of the things we looked for when we bought our family car. That was *pretty cool* for me to hear!

Various home improvement projects—It always seemed like we had something that either needed repair in our home or, at other times, something we wanted to upgrade. I happen to like doing house projects myself, so I started to include my kids in the projects I took on. For example, my daughter's room was ready to be upgraded from the little princess bedroom to a bigger girl room when she was fourteen and about to go to high school. We needed to buy items, including paint, a new ceiling fan, and new furniture. Together, my daughter and I developed the list of items and their approximate costs, which, in turn, controlled our spending, especially when it came time to buy the furniture. Once we were in the store, it was tempting to buy furniture that was more expensive than what we had projected, but because we had a planned budget, it was easier for us to stay on target.

Charitable giving around the holidays—Every year our family reflects on how blessed we are as a family. Although we all contribute to charities throughout the year, around the holidays we have always taken the time to examine if there are things we can do for the less fortunate. We made this practice a part of our family's traditions.

As a family, we found that it was not always only about the financial aspect of the charity but also the time commitment we could make. For example, one year around Christmas, we participated in a charity called Angel Tree Christmas. This charity's focus is to provide kids whose families are going through hardship with Christmas presents that they otherwise would most likely not receive. Each of our kids selected a card from the tree that stated the age of the child and what that child was hoping to receive for Christmas. Two of the requests were for basic essentials like shoes and clothing items. The third request, from an eight-year-old girl, was for a doll.

With the requests in hand, we went shopping for the gifts that each child requested, then wrapped and returned them to the charity. During the process, we discussed how those children might feel on Christmas morning because of our children's generosity. What amazed me was that each of our kids spent more than their normal charity budget that month on the gifts for their child. On Christmas morning, they commented that they hoped their gifts were special for their Angel Tree Christmas kids.

As with the above examples, Money Athletics adventure trips are a great tool to help teach and reinforce money concepts based on real-life events your children will continue to experience as they grow into young adults. Your list of activities may have some similarities to our family, but you will also probably have differences between your list and that of our family. The main point here is to engage actively with your tweens about financial decisions that they will likely experience as they grow older. Not only will it develop their confidence to make those types of money decisions, but all of you may also develop other selective skills along the way.

MONTHLY REVIEW MEETINGS

Another key to strength training for your tween's money fitness is the area of monthly review meetings. As stated in chapter 3, establishing a monthly meeting serves as a good "touchpoint" when your tween and you can balance your checking and savings accounts. This is an opportunity for you to provide guidance and answer any questions about the previous month's spending as well as discuss if there are any upcoming events in the next month that your tween may need help with. These meetings helped all my kids gain an understanding of the various bank statements and how to balance their accounts.

Although I started out having these meetings monthly with my kids, it did not take long before we were skipping our monthly meeting and only meeting every other month, and then just once a quarter. This reduction in the frequency of our meetings started to happen after just six months into the program. The reason for reducing the frequency of the meetings was that my kids were doing so well on their own that meeting every month was no longer required. I still checked in and asked each month if there was anything that they wanted to discuss about their finances and if they might be planning for a big purchase. I wanted them to know that I was always there to help them.

This reduction in the frequency of meetings will likely happen with your tweens as well, and you should take it as a good sign. It means they are grasping how to manage their own money. You will still want them to know that you are always available for impromptu meetings or questions. Even today, while my kids are now young adults, I still ask them questions and have discussions with them almost once every few months. I do that to let them know I am there to help. It also lets them know that I am still approachable regarding their money issues.

FUTURE BIG-TICKET ITEMS

One area that people frequently ask about relates to determining the right time to discuss future big-ticket items with tweens, especially regarding the topic of college and the purchase of a car. I generally recommend restricting the conversation with tweens about college to the importance of saving as much as they can for college.

College has become difficult to afford for many families, and there are many things to consider. In addition to the expense of college, there are considerations such as what they will study, where they might go, whether they'll attend public or private schools, how they might pay for it, whether they might receive scholarships, and so much more. Those more detailed conversations are much better to have with your tweens when they are in high school. An important note to highlight, though, is that when we did have those conversations with our kids in high school, they had a lot more understanding for the situation because they had a solid financial base of knowledge. As a result, we were able to develop a great plan together. I cover this topic in more detail in *Money All-Stars*.

The second big-ticket item that often comes up is the purchase of a car after they get their driver's license. Similar to my recommendation about college, I think it is important to discuss the need to save for a car and possibly set aside one of the savings accounts to help with that. However, having detailed discussions about the specific car, cost of gas, insurance, and maintenance is premature for kids in their tween years. This is another topic covered in *Money All-Stars*.

CHAPTER CHECKLIST

✓ Begin to pay attention to commercials and advertisements you see on TV, in newspapers and magazines, and online that would make for good financial conversations. Keep a running list of commercials that you see so when they come on and your kids are present, you can talk about them together.

✓ Keep your eyes and ears open for natural learning opportunities that happen organically in your day-to-day lives. Activities such as watching TV, shopping online, reading a magazine, or even seeing billboard signs can become learning opportunities. Events such as household repairs provide the opportunity to consider how, when, and where you spend money.

✓ Begin to think of potential Money Athletics adventure trips you can take with your tween. Ideas are available on the website MoneyAthletics.com to get you started.

✓ Schedule your review meetings monthly for at least the first six months. You can be flexible after that, but I encourage you to continue to have at least quarterly meetings until your kids go to college or move out of the house.

✓ Although big-ticket items may come up in conversations with your tween, it is premature to get into the details of such items until your son or daughter is older. Be patient. It is good to discuss the need to save, but the details will likely evolve as they get older.

THE REPLAY

Congratulations, you've arrived at the final chapter of *Money Athletics: Your Game Plan to a Financially Fit Tween*. You now have the entire game plan for developing a financially fit tween. However, the journey for your son or daughter does not end here. In fact, the journey toward young adulthood will continue in all aspects of development. As your tweens' guide in navigating through life, you have the opportunity to substantially influence how financially fit they become as they grow from tweens into teenagers and ultimately into young adults. Along the way, you'll also be able to help as they encounter many other life lessons.

The Money Athletics Program was developed to continue to assist you and your children on their financial journey, so let's take a final look at the key concepts we've covered. I encourage you to come back to this recap anytime you want a quick refresher.

THE LEARNING CHALLENGE

Learning new skills and making them "stick" is a challenge for all of us. Without reinforcement, our knowledge and skill level will return close to our starting point.

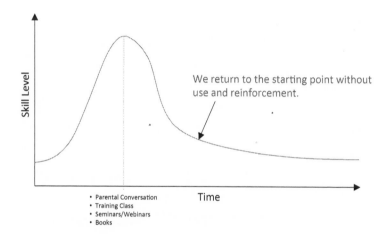

Intuitively, most of us already know this. The key to helping your tween grow toward financial fitness is to break the cycle and not only help your tween learn financial skills but also maintain and grow them.

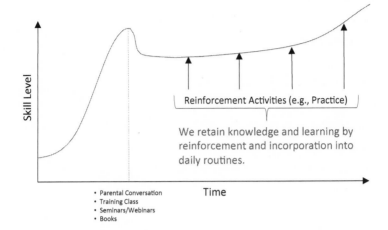

The 70:20:10 model, which is an integral part of the Money Athletics Program, breaks down as follows:

- 70 percent—Dedicated to performing the tasks or activity (doing)
- 20 percent—Coaching and mentoring (feedback and guidance)
- 10 percent—Coursework and training (absorbing)

The key here is that we learn by doing. We can't simply take a class or learn from a teacher and become an instant expert. We have to practice, learn, practice, and learn some more.

How does all of this learning take place for your tween? With you as his or her coach. Although it may be a bit scary, the role you play in coaching your son or daughter to become financially fit begins with you being actively involved. It is essential that you play an active part!

SETTING THE PLAYING FIELD

With the foundation of learning understood, it's time to set the playing field for your tween. The first consideration is to identify when might be the appropriate time to begin this program with your tween. The focus of this program is for kids between the ages of eleven and fourteen. However, it will be your intuition that offers the biggest insights as to the ideal time to get started. A key deciding factor is whether your son or daughter seems ready. If you are on the fence about readiness, thinking about the following scenarios will help reveal your "gut knowledge" related to their readiness.

- Does your son or daughter consistently want to buy things from stores, iTunes, and the Internet? An answer of yes to this question could mean he or she is ready.

- Is your son or daughter knowledgeable about money already, maybe because you have been providing an allowance and teaching some of the financial basics? If yes, this may be a good indicator that he or she is ready. If the answer is no, you may find that your son or daughter is still ready, but you will most likely need to spend more time teaching the financial basics, like balancing an account and understanding the concept of interest, particularly since interest deposits will appear on the accounts.

- With regard to nonmonetary readiness factors, do you believe that your son or daughter has the mental capacity for this responsibility? For instance, are chores done without continual reminders or potential consequences? Is homework done without the need for you to be on his or her case to get it done? What other types of responsibilities are managed by your tween within and outside of your home?

Responses to questions such as these will reveal your son's or daughter's willingness, readiness, and previous experience with being responsible. However, what do you do if the answers are not clear and definitive? Remember, we are discussing the correct age to start this program, not whether you *should* start it. For that reason, if you clearly do not feel your son or daughter is ready, then wait six months and reevaluate. If you are on the fence, I suggest you move forward and implement the program because the benefits will far outweigh the risks.

An essential component to the entire program is finding the right bank or credit union to use when setting up the accounts that will allow your tween to track, manage, and carry out banking activities electronically. Ideally, the financial institution that you bank with will also work for your son or daughter. Whichever institution you choose, it will need to allow the following accounts to be opened for your tween:

1. Savings accounts
2. Checking account
3. Debit card (Visa or Mastercard)
4. Online banking
5. Mobile apps

Once you determine the bank or credit union that your son or daughter will use, you will need to identify the accounts to be established on their behalf:

1. Checking account
2. Visa/Mastercard debit card
3. Savings account #1
4. Savings account #2 for injury prevention
5. Savings account #3 for charity (optional)
6. Savings Account #4 for special long-term items (optional)
7. Investment/college savings account (optional)

With the accounts determined, it's time to identify the frequency of regular family review meetings. Starting out with monthly meetings is optimal for several reasons:

1. Most bank statements are issued on a monthly basis, and it is easiest to review a single month of bank statements versus multiple months at one time.
2. Enough time will have passed, typically about four weeks, which is an ample amount of time for you to review your tween's progress and address any issues that may have surfaced, such as fees, unbalanced accounts, and his or her efforts toward future goals.
3. Because you also will receive your statements on a monthly basis, it will help you bond with your son or daughter over a grown-up activity. Be sure to compliment your tweens on the things they are doing right and encourage them in the areas where they may need help.

As you and your tween progress, you can reevaluate whether a less frequent meeting schedule will be sufficient. It's essential that, no matter the frequency, a regular schedule be maintained. Mistakes and issues will occur, and having an agreed-upon time to meet and discuss them will be helpful in resolving issues before they have a chance to get out of hand.

The role of chores and how they apply to the program is an area of concern for most parents. This is also an area where there are many different philosophies. Remember, the point of the Money Athletics Program is to help your tweens grow into financially fit young adults, not to make them do chores. That being said, I certainly see the dilemma.

In our family, we took the stance that everyone was required to do certain chores as a member of the family. We all shared in those responsibilities, and nobody could escape from helping out. Those responsibilities started for our kids at a young age, so they were used to what was expected from them long before they started with the Money Athletics Program. However, our kids did go through a phase when getting them to do their chores became a constant challenge. We began to apply a "service fee" when we were not able to correct a behavior related to a particular chore. This was an effective motivator for our children and may be equally effective for yours, since none of us likes the consequence of having money taken out of an account for something we've failed to do.

The Baseline Expense Plan

With the accounts identified and the process outlined, the next step is to determine the details of the baseline expense plan, which focuses on what your tween will be financially responsible to pay throughout the year. Downloadable worksheets are available at MoneyAthletics.com to help you through this process. Items to consider include the following:

- Allowance and entertainment
- Clothing and shoes
- Birthday party gifts to friends
- Hot lunches at school
- School supplies

At a minimum, your list of items should match those listed above, but you may also want to include other items. The above items are good baseline items that are relevant to tweens. It is important to not overallocate money toward the above items since you want to encourage your tweens to think about their spending habits. When they become teenagers, not overallocating to these items may also encourage them to get a job to help supplement their finances.

The total of the above items signifies how much your tween will be responsible for managing annually. The next area to look at is how often you will pay your son or daughter, such as monthly, weekly, or a timeframe that matches how often you receive your paycheck. We chose monthly since that seemed to match with our monthly family review meetings.

Two additional areas to keep at the forefront are smartphones and extra projects. In our family, we paid for our tweens' smartphones and the family's smartphone plan, but our tweens were responsible for any lost or broken smartphones and the associated deductibles that had to be paid to replace a phone. This ensured that they had some skin in the game.

Extra projects are tasks that come up outside of your tween's normal chores. These can be considered as opportunities for extra payments. Your son or daughter will appreciate the extra income, and you will appreciate having the project completed.

One of the other key points to keep in mind is that although this program helps your children begin to have some financial responsibility and independence, it is OK for you to treat them on occasion. Giving to your children is one of the honors of being a parent. However, be sure to separate those "treats" from items they should pay for. There may come a time when your tweens try to convince you to pay for something that has become their responsibility. If and when such a situation arises, have fun with it. Call them on it and smile.

THE BASELINE FUTURE PLAN

Understanding and getting into the practice of paying yourself first is an essential element to the overall Money Athletics Program. The benefits from your tween developing a habit around this concept will place him or her far ahead of other young adults with regard to financial fitness. There are four types of accounts that will contribute to your son's or daughter's future goals and aspirations—each in a different way. They include the following:

Injury prevention account—This is your tween's emergency fund account that will provide a safety net when unforeseen financial events occur. I consider this a "must have" account.

Long-term savings account—This account can be used for a variety of purposes, depending on your tween's future goals. Those goals will likely change, so this account should simply be there for future goals, whatever they may become. I also believe this is an important "must have" account.

401(k) account—This can be another savings account or an investment or college savings account. If you wish to do so, you can include a matching approach to benefit your tween. I like the idea of using this account for retirement since it provides for an early start that is about ten to fifteen years earlier than most financial advisers recommend. The concepts around this account can also spark fun and entertaining conversations with your tween by giving him or her the opportunity to dream about how large the accounts could grow by retirement time. This is an optional account but one that I highly recommend you consider.

Charity account—Giving to a charity, or multiple charities, is the purpose of this account. Although this account is not specifically focused on growing the financial wealth of your tween, it certainly will help him or her grow empathy toward others. Again, this is an optional account; however, I highly encourage establishing one if giving to charity is an important value within your family.

The percentage amounts to fund each of these accounts will vary based on your specific family and financial considerations. In our family, we funded each of these accounts with a 10 percent allocation. I recommend at least 5 percent if possible.

Opening Day—The Rollout

In preparing for opening day, you bring all of the details of the Money Athletics Program together and devise how you will roll out the plan to your son or daughter. Using the baseline expense plan and the baseline future plan, you will determine the gross salary to pay your tween, the interval for payments, and all of the allocation values for each account. There are also downloadable worksheets at MoneyAthletics. com that will help you through these calculations.

Once you complete the calculations, it is time to begin the rollout process. The first part of this is the offer letter, which is used to explain the specifics of the program to your son or daughter. The offer letter is also a tool to get your tween excited. Most likely, this will be the first offer letter your child will have ever received, so make it a big deal and plan to make the presentation of this letter exciting and celebratory. Your tween is about to start the journey to becoming a financially fit young adult.

Another action item during the rollout process is to identify the name of the company you want to create for your family's program. Although you're welcome to use the name "Money Athletics," it could be fun to brainstorm and come up with a name that is meaningful to your son or daughter and your entire family. You can make the task of brainstorming your company name part of the initial rollout meeting or set aside a time shortly thereafter to meet and identify a name.

After you complete the offer process and determine a company name, the next step is to set up the accounts. The offer letter you created should summarize the accounts needed. This will result in your first Money Athletics adventure trip with your tween. Your son or daughter will need to be with you when you go to the bank or credit union to complete the paperwork and set up the accounts. Your tween will definitely feel more grown-up as you complete this paperwork process together. Remember that you will need to be a cosigner on the accounts. When you establish the accounts, make sure you have online access to all of the accounts that you establish. That will be necessary for the rest of the setup process.

Once your accounts are set up at the bank or credit union, you should be able to access them online to set up the appropriate automatic transfers according to the desired payroll schedule you plan to use for your tween, such as monthly.

About a week after the accounts have been set up, you will receive the debit card and checks for your tween's accounts. That is the perfect time to do the next three adventure trips. The first one is to go to the bank and show your son or daughter how to deposit money. The second is to visit the ATM machine to do a cash withdrawal and a review of the other ATM features. The last one is to go to a store so your tween has the opportunity to use the debit card in making a purchase. Each one of these trips will be a fun and exciting learning experience for your tween.

YOU IN THE ROLE OF COACH

Now that the program details have been worked out, your role as your son's or daughter's coach begins. Being a coach can seem like a daunting task, but it doesn't have to be if you keep your focus on the following five key areas:

1. Coaches understand and build confidence.
2. Coaches should be tough but fair.
3. Coaches teach life skills, not just money skills.
4. Coaches should never be demeaning.
5. Coaches make mistake too.

Each of these areas is already an aspect of your role as a parent. With regard to the Money Athletics Program, you are now applying them to your role as a financial coach.

STRENGTH TRAINING

Learning opportunities can present themselves either naturally or through planned activities that we call adventure trips. Natural learning opportunities are the ones that are always around us and occur spontaneously, whether while watching TV, reading a magazine, browsing the Internet, or through interactions with others. As you become more alert to such opportunities, you will be amazed at how often natural situations present themselves. Engaging in a conversation with your son or daughter when these moments occur will prove invaluable to your tween's financial fitness journey.

It is also optimal to set up learning scenarios that help set the stage to expose your tween to specific topics. Some examples include gift-giving, planning a vacation trip, purchasing a new family vehicle, and even home improvement projects. You will also find a reference list of adventure trips on the MoneyAthletics.com website to help spark some ideas for you. Remember that since your tween learns best by doing, it is important to present real-life opportunities, either naturally or through your planned adventures.

◎ ◎ ◎

Congratulations again on beginning this journey with your tweens and supporting them as they move toward financial fitness. This is an exciting adventure to embark upon with them. As you proceed together on this journey, I believe you will see your tweens grow in amazing ways.

Keep in mind that you are not alone as you move through this program. Support for you and your tweens' success is always available to you. There are additional resources at MoneyAthletics.com that you may want to use and reference periodically. This includes coaching services, downloadable templates and worksheets, blogs and articles relevant to you and your tween, and even comments and feedback from other parents. In addition, remember that this book is part of the Moneyletics MAP Series that provides guidance for you as your children progress through the various ages to adulthood. The Moneyletics MAP Series includes the following:

- Money Amateurs Program (for young kids to age ten)

- Money Athletics Program (for tweens from ages eleven to fourteen)

- Money All-Stars Program (for teenagers from ages fifteen to eighteen)

- Money All-Stars Plus (for young adults from age eighteen forward)

◎ ◎ ◎

Let me leave you with one final thought. There is an African proverb that says, "If you want to go fast, go alone. If you want to go far, go together." Each of my children has amazed me with regard to his or her financial awareness. All have gone further than I could have ever imagined when we started on our financial fitness journey together. I firmly believe that the successes they are enjoying are because we did this as a team using the principles in the Moneyletics MAP Series. With your guidance, how far might your son or daughter go?

ACKNOWLEDGMENTS

Eighteen months ago, I met with Polly Letofsky to inquire about the feasibility of writing a book to help parents raise their kids into financially fit young adults. I received encouragement from many friends and family, but doubts remained. Polly, you helped me past those doubts and guided me to get this project off the ground—and for that I will always be grateful.

Donna Mazzitelli, my exceptional writing coach and editor, helped me through the roller coaster ride that writing a book can be. Your feedback, guidance, collaboration, and patience were always the right amount and just what I needed. I can't thank you enough for your role in this project!

Thank you to my wonderful wife, Karen. You always thought that this was a book I needed to write, and you were always encouraging. I love you, BOO!

To my wonderful kids, Scott, Nicole, and Tyler. Although you all play starring roles in this book, it is your role as my kids that has provided me inspiration that goes beyond words. For that I am forever grateful.

To Roni Lambrecht. Your journey as an author for your book *Parenting at Your Best* provided me a consistent beacon throughout this project of what great parenthood looks like. Thank you for sharing your moving and inspirational writings!

To all my friends who encouraged the writing of this book, I thank you!

ABOUT THE AUTHOR

Craig Kaley, married to his wife, Karen, since 1993, loves being a parent to his two sons and daughter, and like many parents, he has a passionate desire to leave a lasting legacy for them. That includes financial fitness.

While his kids were young, what he wanted was a way to help them learn life skills around managing money. He was looking for a parenting tool that went beyond simply teaching financial topics. When he couldn't find what he was looking for, he created the system that became the Moneyletics MAP Series.

Athletics and the outdoors are a big part of the Kaley family. Craig was a coach for his kids' sports teams of soccer and baseball while his wife, Karen, was often the team mom.

Craig was able to carry his experience as an inspiring athletic coach to the topic of finances. Principles of education, coaching, practicing, and real-life execution are foundational elements of the program.

Possessing an engineering degree and MBA, Craig believes his role as a parent has contributed the most to this endeavor to create the Moneyletics MAP Series. The proof is witnessing his three kids, and the kids of many other families who have gone through the program, acquire the financial skills that make parents proud.

Today, Craig is a practicing IT professional and a speaker, trainer, and coach for Moneyletics. His desire to leave a legacy has expanded to help as many parents as he can in raising their kids to become financially fit young adults.